BASIC INSTRUCTOR GUITAR VOL.1 by Jerry Snyder

D1410406

about the course
Volume I

BASIC INSTRUCTOR GUITAR, Vol. I, Student Edition (revised) is designed for individual instruction or for the guitar class. The revised edition includes *pickstyle* accompaniment techniques. This course includes basic instruction in *chords, strums, pickstyle techniques, fingerstyle techniques,* and *songs,* along with a *solo* and *ensemble* approach to learning music notation. All basics and fundamentals of music are included - plus theory.

The book is divided into two sections: **Section One** - chords, theory, songs and accompaniment; **Section Two** -music fundamentals, notation, solos and ensembles. Each section is organized in a learning sequence that goes from the easy to the more difficult. **Study and learn the material in these two sections *concurrently*.** Develop your own learning sequence by combining a **balance** of material from each section. You have the *option* to learn either or both **pickstyle** and **fingerstyle** guitar techniques. Use the SongKey / Rating Index to vary the song sequence and to discover songs in the book that are within your "chording" ability.

BASIC INSTRUCTOR GUITAR, Vol. I, Teacher's Edition contains a course overview, units of study, supplementary teaching suggestions and materials, a chord and fingerboard chart, drawings of right hand strumming and plucking techniques - plus a demonstration record of the strums and ensembles contained in the student book.

Volume II

BASIC INSTRUCTOR GUITAR, Vol. II, Student Edition contains additional accompaniment techniques such as those used in bluegrass, calypso, latin strums, bossa-nova, ragtime, running bass patterns and hammers. The book includes instruction and application of the *secondary chords, moveable chords, extensions, alterations and substitutions.* Using a *solo* and *ensemble* approach to learning music notation, students review first position notes and learn to play in third and fifth position.

BASIC INSTRUCTOR GUITAR, Vol. II, Teacher's Edition contains units of study, course objectives, charts on strums and moveable chords plus a wealth of supplementary teaching suggestions and materials. The book includes a record which contains the strums, finger patterns and solos and ensembles found in the student book.

about the author

Jerry Snyder combines his knowledge of the guitar with a backbround as a music educator, coordinator, clinician, arranger and progessional musician. He received his B.A. and M.A. from San Jose State University. Jerry is presently the Performing Arts Coordinator for the East Side Union High School District in San Jose, California. He has pioneered team-teaching of Band, Music and Art Survey, Music in the Humanities and the Guitar Class. He has written, arranged and edited over 100 guitar publications. Write Jerry Snyder, P.O. Box 1167, Los Gatos, CA 95031 for a catalog.

Section One: THE GUITAR

Broadly speaking, there are two types of guitars: 1) steel string guitars, 2) nylon string guitars. Both types may either be *acoustic* (not amplified) or *electric* (amplified). The selection of a guitar is really a matter of personal choice. The essential difference is their tone quality.

STEEL STRING GUITAR

The steel string guitar's distinguishing characteristics are a rather narrow fingerboard, a pick guard and steel stings. The flat-top steel string guitar is a good beginning guitar. The tone color (timbre) is bright, brassy and forceful and lends itself to folk, country, ragtime, blues and pop styles of music. This kind of guitar is generally played pickstyle, but fingerstyle techniques are also commonly used. Never put nylon strings on a steel string guitar. Light guage strings may be used to make depressing the strings easier, fig. 1.

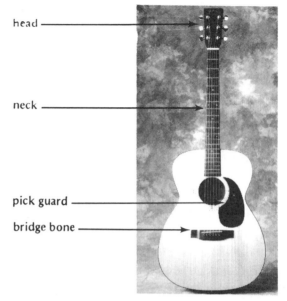

fig. 1 **Steel string flat-top guitar**

NYLON STRING GUITAR

The distinguishing characteristics of the nylon string (classical) guitar are a wide fingerboard, an open peg box (slotted tuning mechanism) and nylon strings. Some student model nylon string guitars have a slightly narrower neck than the tradition classical guitar. The nylon string guitar is an excellent guitar for the beginner. Having less tension on the strings than the steel string guitar, the strings are easy to depress. The tone qualiy is dark, mellow and delicate. This type of guitar has a rich repertoire of classical music and is also a popular choice for folk, latin and jazz. Right hand fingerstyle techniques are generally used on this kind of guitar. Do not put steel strings on a nylon string guitar, fig. 2.

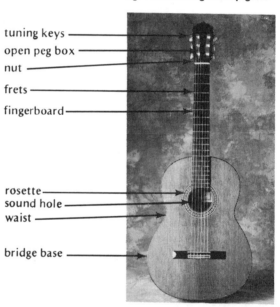

fig. 2 **Nylon string classic type guitar**

ELECTRIC GUITAR

The *solid body* guitar is popular with rock, blues and country musicians. The *semi-hollow body* and *hollow body electric* guitars are popular choices for country, pop, blues and jazz musical styles. These guitars have thin "cut-away" necks designed to enable the player to perform in high positions and volume and tone controls that allow for a wide range of tone (timbre) qualities ranging from very bright to dark. Without an amplifier, these guitars can barely be heard.

An **amplifier** with a minimum of 10 watts is adequate for practice. There are also earphones that run on a nine volt battery that can be plugged directly Into the guitar.

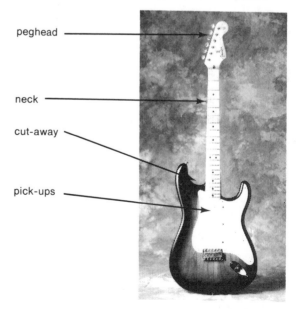

fig. 3. **Solid body electric guitar**

TUNING THE GUITAR

The problem in tuning the guitar lies in the difficulty of matching one musical pitch to another. You usually have the additional distraction of attempting to match the pitch of the guitar to a musical pitch that has a different tone quality (timbre) such as a piano, a pitchpipe or even an open guitar string to a fretted (depressed) guitar string. It will take a while to develop the "sense of pitch" necessary for tuning your guitar. Be patient!

TO A PIANO

Begin with the 6th string (low E). Sound the tone on the piano and using your "tonal memory" match the pitch of the **Open** 6th string to the piano. This may be accomplished by first purposely lowering the open 6th string below desired pitch and while plucking the string with the thumb, slowly turn the appropriate tuning key with your left hand until you have matched the pitch. Tune each string in this manner. Then repeat the entire process. fig. 1.

TO ITSELF

The guitar may be tuned to itself. Either use a tuning fork (E) or estimate the pitch of the 6th string (low 3) and then follow the steps as outlined below. fig. 2.

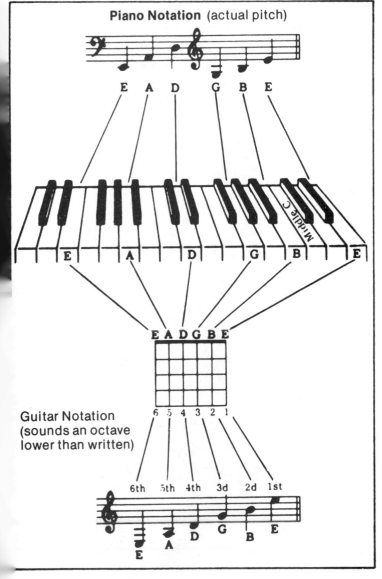

fig. 1 **Tune to the piano**

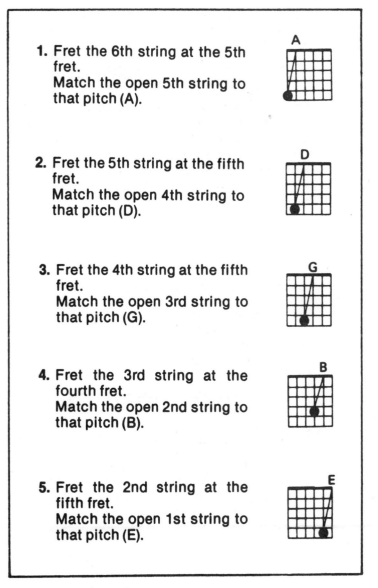

1. Fret the 6th string at the 5th fret.
   Match the open 5th string to that pitch (A).

2. Fret the 5th string at the fifth fret.
   Match the open 4th string to that pitch (D).

3. Fret the 4th string at the fifth fret.
   Match the open 3rd string to that pitch (G).

4. Fret the 3rd string at the fourth fret.
   Match the open 2nd string to that pitch (B).

5. Fret the 2nd string at the fifth fret.
   Match the open 1st string to that pitch (E).

fig. 2 **Tune the guitar to itself**

PLAYING POSITIONS

Playing positions vary somewhat with the type of right hand technique used, the type of guitar played, and the style of music performed. The following is a description of the basic fingerstyle and pickstyle playing positions used on the acoustic and electric guitar.

SITTING POSITION

Cross the right leg over your left and place the waist of the guitar on the right thigh. Tilt the guitar slightly toward you. You should be looking over the end of the fingerboard. The neck is at a 15 degree angle (upward) from the floor. The forearm rests on the edge of the guitar at a point just above the bridge base, fig. 1.

fig. 1 **Sitting position**

CLASSICAL POSITION

Sit erect and forward in a chair. Elevate the left foot by placing it on a footstool. The left knee should be slightly higher than the hip. Place the waist of the guitar on the left thigh. Tilt the guitar slightly toward you. You should be looking over the sound hole at the point where the fingerboard ends. The neck of the guitar is held at about a 20 degree angle (upward) from the floor, fig. 2.

fig. 2 **Classical position**

STANDING POSITION

A strap may be used to hold the guitar when standing. Even in the standing position, the placement of the forearm should be on the edge of the guitar just above the bridge. The strap for the acoustic guitar is attached to an end pin and to the head of the guitar. Electric guitars have a strap button on the body of the guitar in addition to the end pin, fig. 3.

fig. 3 **Standing position**

BEGINNING STRUM

Pickstyle. Use a **pick** (flat-pick, plectrum) to strum the strings. I recommend a medium gauge pear shape or drop shape pick, fig. 1 and 2.

fig. 1 **Pear shape**

fig. 2 **Drop shape**

The pick should be held between the thumb and index finger. Keep the thumb rigid, fig. 3. Place the forearm on the edge of the guitar above the bridge, fig. 4. Strum downward across the strings.

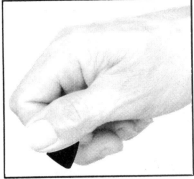
fig.1 **Holding the pick**

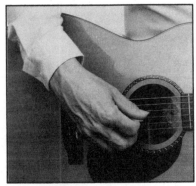
fig. 2 **Arm position**

Fingerstyle. With the forearm resting on the edge of the guitar just above the bridge base, allow the right hand to hang down in a natural manner. The fingers are approximately above the rosette and the thumb is extended toward the sound hole. Keep the fingers slightly curved and bunched together.

Now **brush** (strum) down across the strings (low to high) with the index and middle fingers of the right hand. It is the fingernails that make contact and brush across the strings. The motion of the strum is primarily from the fingers. If the fingers have been properly curved, simply open up the hand and allow the fingers to brush the strings, fig. 5 and 6.

fig. 3 **Arm and hand position**

fig. 4 **Brush strum**

THEORY

The strings to be strumed may either be written as quarter notes or as a slash (**/**). The quarter note and slash receive one count or beat. The curved line (**{**) means to strum the strings. A down-stroke with a pick is indicated by this sign (**⊓**).

Count: 1   2   3   4

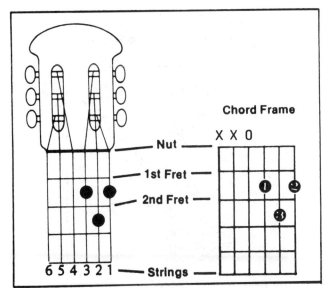

6 5 4 3 2 1 — Strings

fig. 5 **D chord on the guitar fingerboard**

CHORD FRAME NOTATION

The standard chord frame or diagram is used to indicate the position of the fingers of the **left** hand.

The fingers of the left hand are indicated as follows:

1 = index finger
2 = middle finger
3 = ring finger
4 = little finger
x = do not play
0 = open string

KEY OF D

D CHORD

In the Key of D, the D chord operates as "home base." Songs in the Key of D nearly always begin and end on the D chord.

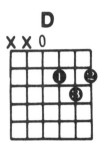

D

X X 0

fig. 1 **Fretboard Analysis**

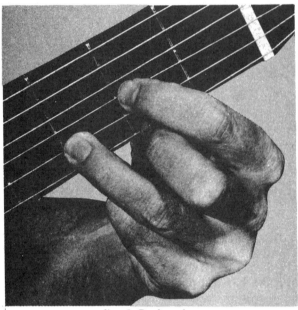

fig. 2 **D chord**

THEORY

The D chord is built upon the first tone (do) of the D scale and is called the Tonic or I Chord.

Place the fingers of the left hand just behind the fret. If the fretted string produces a "buzz," you need to either press more firmly or move the fingers closer toward the fret. The fingernails of the left hand must be short.

A7 CHORD

In the Key of D, the A7 chord plays a dominant role. Notice that most of the songs in the Key of D end with an A7 to D chord progression.

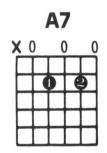

A7

X 0 0 0

fig. 3 **Fretboard Analysis**

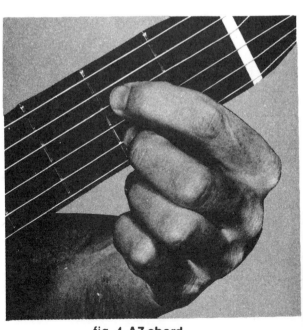

fig. 4 **A7 chord**

THEORY

The A7 chord is built upon the fifth tone (sol) of the D scale and is called the Dominant 7th or V7 chord.

Scale - W W W # W W W H

D Scale

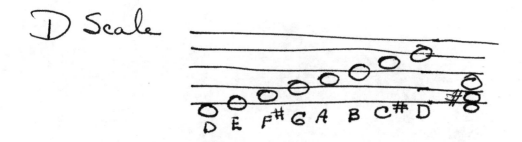

D E F# G A B C# D #

A Scale   A   A¹

A B C# D E F# G# A   E C# A   E C# A G

These directions are for planning purposes only. You may find that construction projects, traffic, or other events may cause road conditions to differ from the map results.

Map data ©2005 NAVTEQ™, Tele Atlas

Using a **Down-stroke** with a pick or a **Brush Strum,** practice the following chord drills. Repeat each drill several times. Each slash (/) represents one count and one strum.

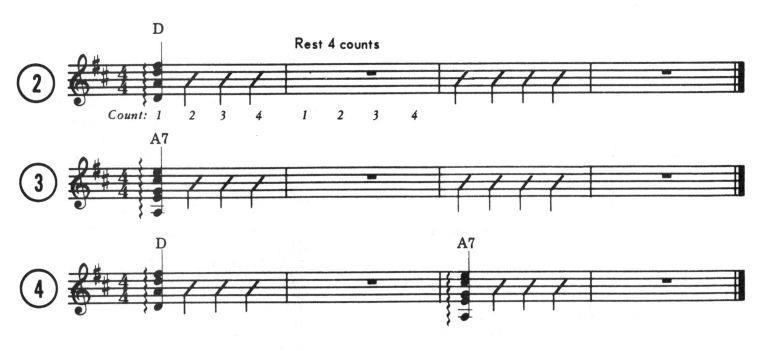

TRANSPORTATION

When changing from the D to the A7, lift fingers of the left hand quickly and simultaneously off the fingerboard. Place the fingers in the new chord position all at once (simultaneously).

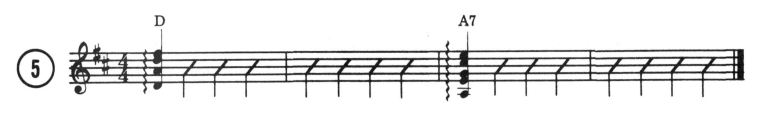

SOME FOLKS DO

Stephen Foster

Some folks like to sigh; some folks do, some folks do.
Some folks get grey hair; some folks do, some folks do.

Some folks long to die,
Brood - ing o - ver cares, } but that's not me nor you.

8

MARY ANN

Traditional

First Note

Moderate

D   A7

All day, all night, Ma - ry Ann, _____

D

Down by the sea - shore sift - ing sand. _____

A7

Ev - en lit - tle chil - dren join in the band _____

D

Down by the sea - shore sift - ing sand. _____

GOOD NEWS

First Note

Lively

Spiritual

D   A7   D

Good News, char-i-ots com-in', Good News, char-i-ots com-in', Good

A7   D

News, char-i-ots com-in' and I don't want it to leave-a-me be-hind.

PRACTICE TIP

Initially, you will have difficulty singing and playing at the same time. Drill the chords and strum separately. Try singing the song without playing the guitar. Now put it together.

HE'S GOT THE WHOLE WORLD IN HIS HANDS

Moderately   Spiritual

CHORUS: He's got the whole world— in His hands,— He's got the
VERSES: 1. He's got the lit-tle bit-ty ba-by in His hands,— He's got the
2. He's got my broth-ers and my sis-ters in His hands,— He's got my
3. He's got ev-'ry-bod-y here in His hands,— He's got —

whole world— in His hands,— He's got the whole world—
lit-tle bit-ty ba - by in His hands,— He's got the lit-tle bit-ty ba - by
broth-ers and my sis-ters in His hands,— He's got my broth-ers and my sis-ters
ev-'ry-bod-y here— in His hands,— He's got — ev-'ry-bod-y here —

in His hands,— He's got the whole world in His hands._____
in His hands,— He's got the whole world in His hands. (Chorus)
in His hands,— He's got the whole world in His hands. (Chorus)
in His hands,— He's got the whole world in His hands. (Chorus)

HEY LOLLY, LOLLY LO

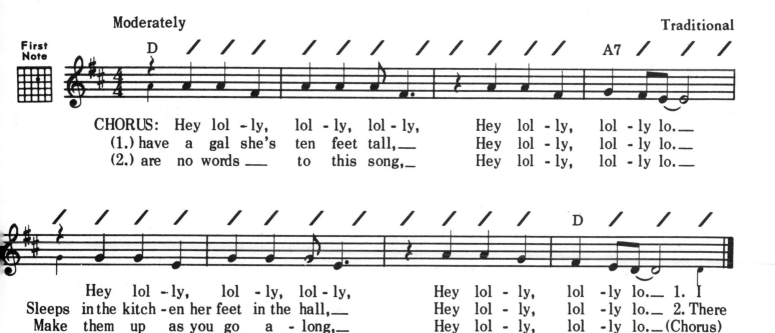

Moderately   Traditional

CHORUS: Hey lol - ly, lol - ly, lol - ly, Hey lol - ly, lol - ly lo.—
(1.) have a gal she's ten feet tall,— Hey lol - ly, lol - ly lo.—
(2.) are no words — to this song,— Hey lol - ly, lol - ly lo.

Hey lol - ly, lol - ly, lol - ly, Hey lol - ly, lol - ly lo.— 1. I
Sleeps in the kitch - en her feet in the hall,— Hey lol - ly, lol - ly lo.— 2. There
Make them up as you go a - long,— Hey lol - ly, lol - ly lo.— (Chorus)

FREE STROKE (Thumb)

Pluck the 4th string with the **thumb.** Allow the thumb to continue to move forward and above the 3rd string. Do not come to rest on the 3rd string, fig. 1 and 2. The motion of the **free stroke** comes from the joint where the thumb joins the hand. Do not bend the thumb at the first joint. In guitar notation, the thumb is indicated with a lower case, italic **p** (pulgar).

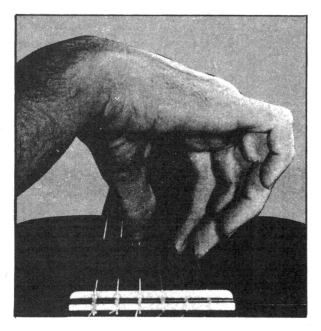

fig. 1 **Preparation for rest stroke**

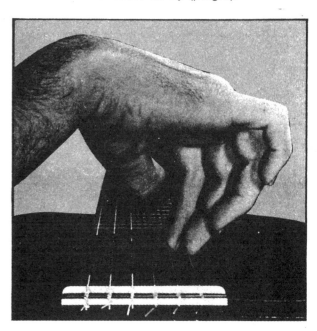

fig. 2 **Completion of rest stroke**

PRIMARY BASS (Root)

Every chord is built upon a foundation or **Root** (R). It is the root of the chord that gives the chord its name. It is the root of the chord that functions as the **Primary Bass.** For example, a D chord has a D (open 4th string) as its root and the A7 chord has an A (open 5th string) as its root. Using a **down-stroke** with a pick or a **free stroke** with the thumb, play the following drill.

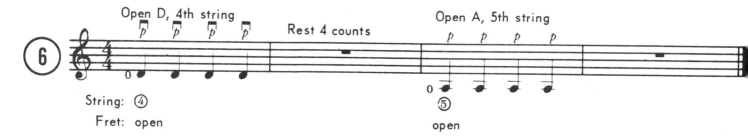

BASS CHORD (Thumb Brush)

In the **Bass Chord** or **Thumb Brush** strum, the root (R) of the chord is played and is followed by three strums downward across the **top three** strings (3rd, 2nd, 1st). Give emphasis (stress) to the root of the chord. Use all down-strokes in pickstyle. In fingerstyle, pluck the root of the chord with the thumb (free stroke) and brush the top strings with the fingers.

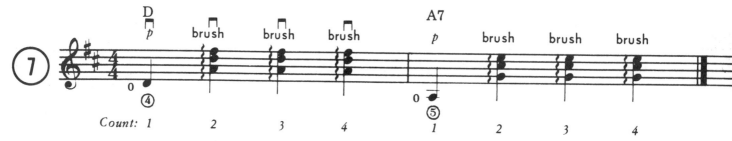

*NOTE: Some teachers may prefer the use of a free stroke with the thumb.
See page 60 for an explanation of the free stroke.*

PUTTIN' ON THE STYLE

Traditional

Lively

CHORUS

Put - tin' on the ag - o - ny, put - tin' on the style,

That's what all the young folks are do - ing all the while, And

as I look a - round me, I'm ver - y apt to smile, To

see so man - y peo - ple put - tin' on the style.

LOVE SOMEBODY, YES I DO

English Folk Song

Moderate

1. Love some-bod - y, yes, I do, Love some-bod - y, yes, I do,
2. Love some-bod - y, can't guess who, Love some-bod - y, can't guess who,
3. Love some-bod - y's smile so true, Love some-bod - y's smile so true,

Love some - bod - y, yes, I do, Love some - bod - y but I won't tell who.
Love some - bod - y, can't guess who, Love some - bod - y but I won't tell who.
Love some - bod - y's smile so true, Love some - bod - y but I won't tell who.

ROCK-A MY SOUL

Moderately   Spiritual

First
Note

D / / /   / / / /   A7 / / /

Rock-a my soul in the bo-som of A - bra - ham, Rock-a my soul in the

/ / / /   D / / /   / / / /

bo-som of A - bra-ham, Rock-a my soul in the bo-som of A - bra - ham

A7 / / /   D / / /   / / / /   / /

Oh, rock-a my soul.   So high, you can't get o - ver it,

A7 / / /   / / / /   D / / /

So low, you can't get un - der it.   So wide, you

/ / / /   A7 / / /   D / /

can't get 'round___ it.   Oh, rock - a my soul.

BASS CHORD (Thumb Brush) 3/4

In pickstyle, use a down-stroke to pluck the primary bass note (the root of the chord) on the first beat of the measure. Strum downward across the top three strings on the second and third beats. In fingerstyle, use the thumb to pluck the root of the chord. The fingers brush down across the strings on beats two and three.

D   A7

String: ④   ⑤
Fret: 0   0
Count: 1   2   3

THEORY

In three-quarter time (3/4), there are three beats in each measure. The first beat should be emphasized or stressed.

DOWN IN THE VALLEY

REVIEW

It is important to establish good habits. Check to see if you are doing the following:

Holding the guitar – Hold it against your body with the upper part of the guitar slightly tilted toward you.

Left arm – Keep the left elbow in close to your body.

Left hand – Keep the wrist out (away from you) and prevent the palm of the hand from touching the neck of the guitar. Position the thumb on the back of the neck slightly past the middle.

Right arm – Rest the forearm on the edge of the guitar just above the saddle.

Right hand – Strum over the rosette.

G CHORD

In the Key of D, the G chord is the third most frequently used chord.

G

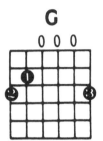

fig. 1 **Fretboard Analysis**

fig. 2 **G chord**

The G chord is built upon the fourth tone (fa) of the D scale and is called the sub-dominant or IV chord.

You will be able to play the G chord without any difficulty if you closely observe the following:

1. Keep the left wrist out.
2. Do not allow the palm of the hand to touch the neck of the guitar.
3. The thumb makes contact with the guitar on the back of the neck — slightly past the middle.
4. By keeping the wrist out, the first and second fingers will angle across the fretboard allowing the third finger to fall easily in place (study photo).
5. The nails of the left hand must be short.

OPTIONAL FINGERINGS

G

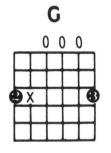

G

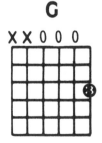

G

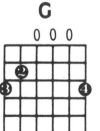

fig. 2 **Some guitarists prefer the "sound" of this G chord. Allow the second finger to deaden (x) the 5th string.**

fig. 3 **A simplified version for the young students. Most beginners should avoid this chord.**

fig. 4 **The most practical fingering when going to and from the C chord. More difficult because of the fourth finger.**

Using a **Down-stroke** or a **Brush Strum**, practice the following drills. Now play the chord changes in *Beautiful Brown Eyes*. Keep a steady beat.

BEAUTIFUL BROWN EYES

Traditional

CHORUS: Beau - ti - ful, beau - ti - ful brown eyes! _____ Beau - ti - ful
1. Wil - lie, my dar - lin' I love you, _____ I love you with

beau - ti - ful brown eyes! _____ Beau - ti - ful, beau - ti - ful
all of my heart. _____ To - mor - row we might have been

brown eyes _____ I'll nev - er love blue eyes a - gain. _____
mar - ried, _____ but ram - blin' has kept us a - part.

16

While holding the G chord with the left hand, play the **bass chord** or **thumb brush** strum. Pluck the root of the chord followed by two down strums.

While holding the G chord with the left hand, play the **thumb brush** strum. The thumb **plucks** the root of the chord followed by two **brush** strums.

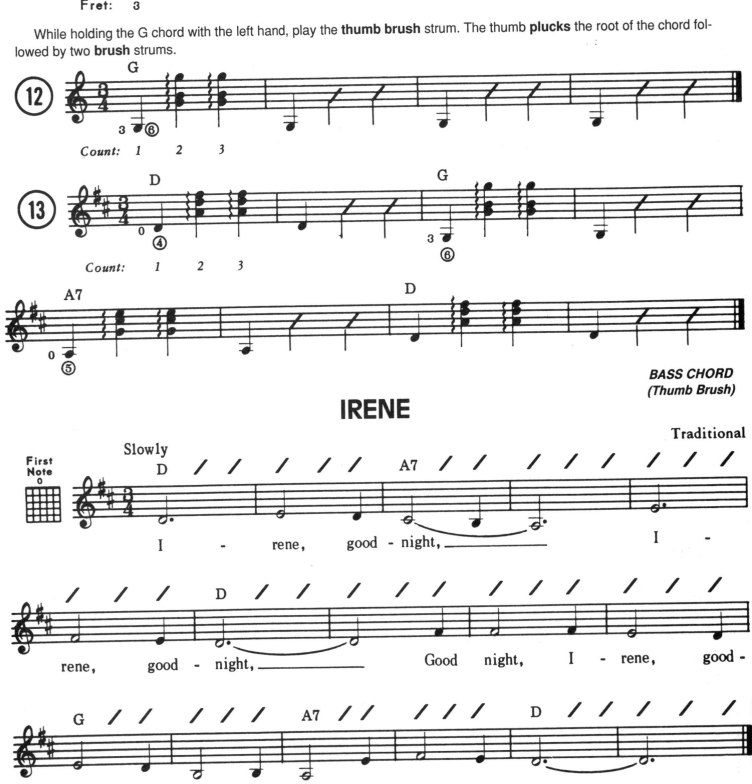

BASS CHORD
(Thumb Brush)

IRENE

Traditional

I - rene, good - night, _____ I -

rene, good - night, _____ Good night, I - rene, good -

night, I - rene, I'll see you in my dreams. _____

BASS CHORD (Thumb Brush) Alternating

Alternate the bass and the strum. Pluck the root of the chord on the first and third beats of the measure. Strum the top three strings of the chord on beats two and four. Use either pickstyle of fingerstyle techiques. The strum should be performed with a **minimum** amount of movement in the right hand and arm.

BANKS OF THE OHIO

BASS CHORD
(Thumb Brush) Alternating

Traditional

Moderately

1. I asked my love to take a walk, to take a walk, just a lit - tle walk. Down be - side, where the wa - ters flow, Down by the banks of the O - hi - o.
2. And on - ly say that you'll be mine, in no oth - er arms, en - twine. Down be - side, where the wa - ters flow, Down by the banks of the O - hi - o.
3. I held a knife a - gainst her breast. As into her arms she pressed. She cried, "Oh Willie don't mur - der me. I'm not pre - pared for e - ter - ni - ty.
4. I start - ed home 'tween twelve and one. I cried, "My God what have I done?" killed the only wom-an I loved. Be - cause she would not be my bride.

KEY OF G

Songs played and sung in the Key of G base their melody and chords on the G scale. The G chord now functions as "home base" or as the Tonic and I chord.

THEORY

The PRIMARY chords in the Key of G are G, C and D7. They are built on the first, fourth and fifth tones of the scale.

fig. 1 **Keyboard Analysis — G scale and primary chords**

D7 CHORD

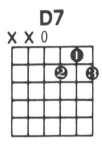

fig. 2 **Fretboard Analysis**

THEORY

The D7 chord is built upon the fifth tone (sol) of the G scale and is called the dominant 7th or V7 chord.

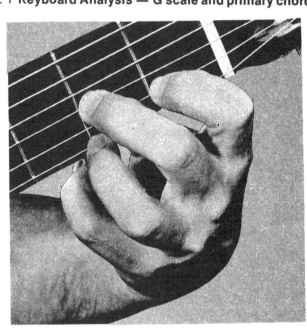

fig. 3 **D7 chord**

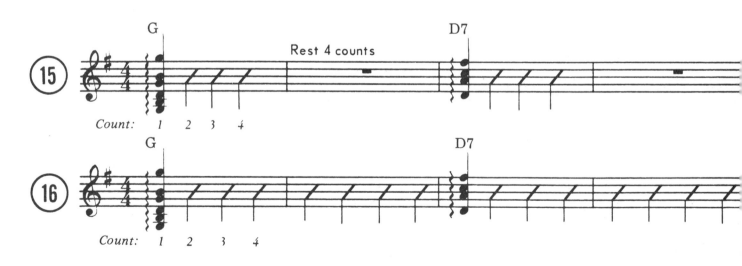

TRANSPORTATION

When changing from the G to the D7 or D7 to G, slide the third finger of the left hand on the 1st string. Do not lift the third finger from the string.

TOM DOOLEY

Moderately

American

CHORUS: Hang down_ your head, Tom Doo-ley, Hang down_ your head and cry.
1. Met her ____ on the moun-tain, swore she'd ____ be my wife.
2. This time ____ to-mor-row, reck-on ____ where I'll be

Hang down_ your head, Tom · Doo-ley, Poor boy_ you're bound_ to die.
But ____ the gal re-fused me, stabbed her ____ with _ a knife.
down in _ some lone-some val-ley, hang-in' from a white_oak tree.

THEORY

ll the songs you have played in the Key of D may be played in the Key of G. *Good News* played in the Key of G
ill sound higher. Changing a song to a new key is called Transposition.

GOOD NEWS

Spiritual

Good News, char-i-ots com-ing, Good

News, char-i-ots com-ing, Good News,

char-i-ots com-in' and I don't want it to leave a-me be-hind.

Transpose *Some Folks Do, Mary Ann, Rock-A My Soul* and *Down In The Valley* to the Key of G. Substitute
he G and D7 chords for the D and A7 chords.

PICK A BALE OF COTTON

Brightly

Traditional

1. Got to jump down, turn a - round, pick a bale of cot - ton, got to
2. Me and my part - ner can pick a bale of cot - ton _____

jump down, turn a - round, pick a bale a day, Got to jump down, turn a - round,
Me and my part - ner can pick a bale a day, _____ Me and my part - ner can

pick a bale of cot - ton, got to jump down, turn a - round, pick a bale a day.
pick a bale of cot - ton, _____ Me and my part - ner can pick a bale a day.

CHORUS

Oh, Law - dy, pick a bale of cot - ton, _____

Oh, Law - dy, pick a bale a day. Oh, Law - dy,

pick a bale of cot - ton. ___ Oh, Law - dy, pick a bale to - day.

THEORY

Transpose this song to the Key of D. Substitute
the D and A7 chords for the G and D7 chords.

PICK A BALE OF COTTON

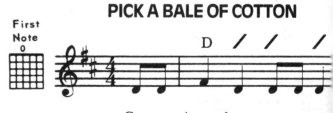

Got to jump down, turn a-rou

BASS DOWN-UP (Thumb Scratch)

In pickstyle, stroke the root (R) of the chord, then strum **down** (⊓) across the 3rd, 2nd and 1st strings (low to high), and then strum **up** (∨) across the 1st and 2nd strings (high to low).

In fingerstyle, a **Scratch** technique is used to strum the strings. The **scratch** technique is performed with the index finger of the right hand. The **scratch** may be performoed either as a **downward** or as an **upward** strum. Pluck the root (R) of the chord with the thumb (p), next scratch down across the top three strings, now scratch up with the fleshy part of the finger across the 1st and 2nd strings. The motion of the strum is from the finger. Do not move the hand out of its basic position above the strings.

RHYTHM

Up to this point, all of the strums have been played on the downbeat. The downbeat is the regularly recurring pulsation in the music. Now divide the beat in half and strum or scratch up on the upbeat (an).

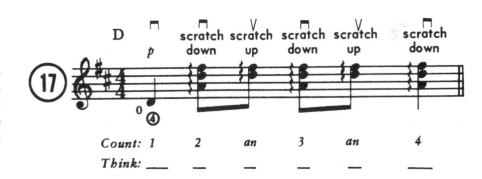

BASS DOWN-UP
(Thumb Scratch)

THIS TRAIN IS BOUND FOR GLORY

C CHORD

In the Key of G, the C chord is the third most frequently used chord.

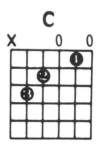

fig. 1 **Fretboard Analysis**

fig. 2 **C chord**

THEORY

The C chord is built upon the fourth tone (fa) of the G scale and is called the Sub-Dominant or IV chord.

Using a **Down-stroke** or a **Brush Strum**, practice the following drill several times.

TRANSPORTATION

When going from the C to the D7 or from the D7 to the C chord, keep the index finger of the left hand down.

Although the weakness of the fourth finger will present a problem in the beginning, the alternate fingering of the G chord is faster and easier when going to and from the C chord. Learn to use this fingering.

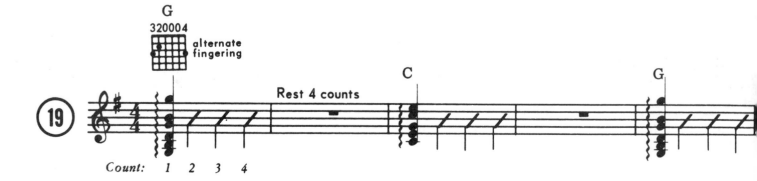

WORRIED MAN BLUES

GIVE ME THAT OLD TIME RELIGION

In the C chord, the **Root** (primary bass note) is located on the 5th string, third fret. Using a **Down-stroke** with a pick or a **Free Stroke** with the thumb, play the following drill. Hold each note for four counts.

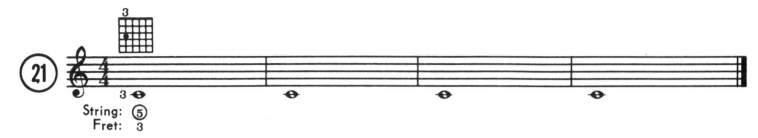

String: ⑤
Fret: 3

While holding the C chord with the left hand, **pluck** the root of the chord and then **strum** three times. Use either pickstyle or fingerstyle techniques.

After you are able to play and sing *Study War No More,* try using a **Bass Chord** or **Thumb Brush** strum. Pluck the root of the chord on the first beat of each measure. The root is located on the 6th string, third fret for the G chord and on the open 4th string for the D7 chord.

BASS CHORD
(Thumb Brush)

STUDY WAR NO MORE

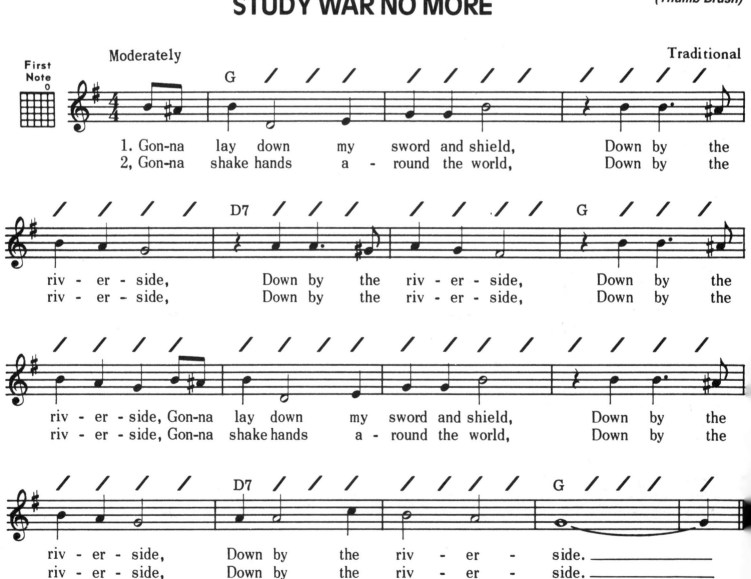

Traditional

1. Gon-na lay down my sword and shield, Down by the
2. Gon-na shake hands a - round the world, Down by the

riv - er - side, Down by the riv - er - side, Down by the
riv - er - side, Down by the riv - er - side, Down by the

riv - er - side, Gon-na lay down my sword and shield, Down by the
riv - er - side, Gon-na shake hands a - round the world, Down by the

riv - er - side, Down by the riv - er - side. _____
riv - er - side, Down by the riv - er - side. _____

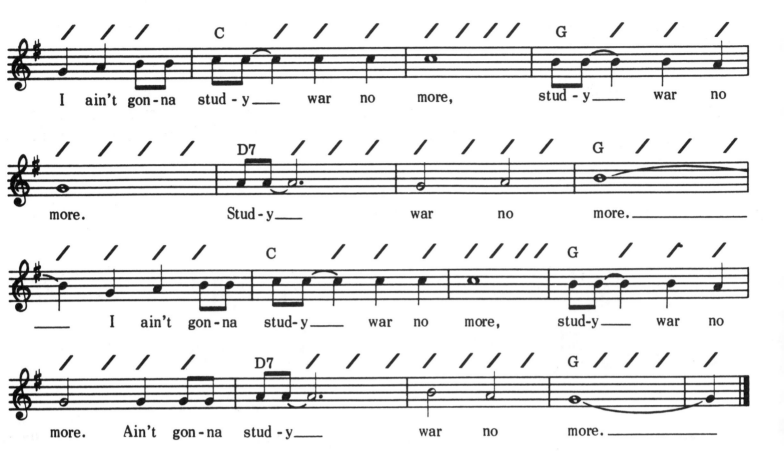

I ain't gon-na stud-y____ war no more, stud-y____ war no more. Stud-y____ war no more.____ ____ I ain't gon-na stud-y____ war no more, stud-y____ war no more. Ain't gon-na stud-y____ war no more.____

BASS DOWN-UP (Thumb Scratch) Alternating

While holding the chord with the left hand, alternate between the **root** and a **down-up strum.** The strum should be performed with a **minimum** amount of movement in the right hand. Keep the right hand and arm from moving too far out of position. Use a down-stroke pick on the root with alternating down-up strokes on the chords or pluck the root of the chord with the thumb followed by a down-up scratch with the index finger.

⊓ = down strum   V = up strum

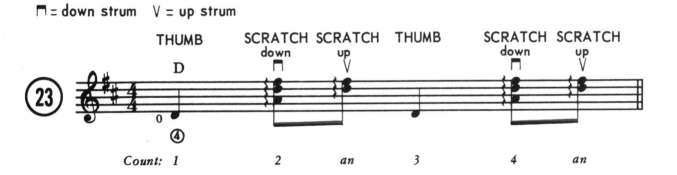

Now apply the **Bass Down-Up** or **Thumb Scratch Alternating** strum to the G, C and D7 chords. When you have the strum "grooved," apply it to *Study War No More.* It is often helpful to practice strums on **open** strings so that you can concentrate on the **right hand** technique.

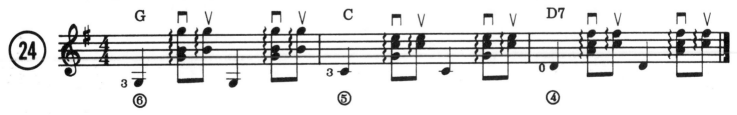

ALTERNATE BASS (Fifth)

In all previous strums, you have plucked the root (R) or **Primary** bass note of the chord. It is possible to achieve a more interesting bass pattern by **alternating** between the root (R) and the fifth (5) of the chord. The **Fifth** (5) is the most frequently used **Alternate Bass.**

Pluck the root (R) on the 1st beat of the measure, strum the top three strings on the 2nd, pluck the fifth (5) on the 3rd beat and strum the strings on 4th. This pattern remains the same for all chords. Drill each chord.

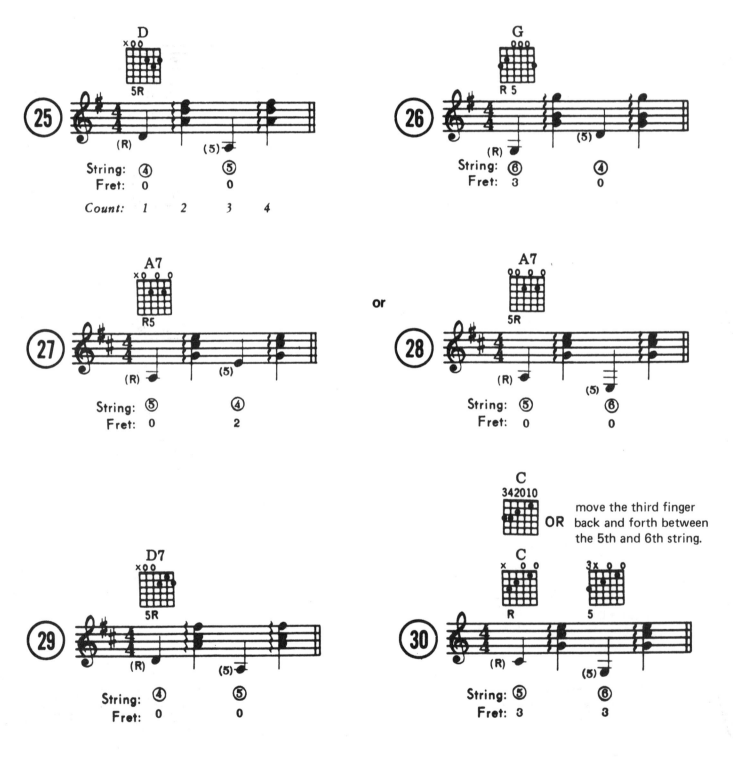

Memorize where the root and fifth are located on each chord. "Groove" the strum and apply it to familiar songs. Review *Banks Of The Ohio, He's Got The Whole World, Tom Dooley, Worried Man Blues* using the **Alternate Bass Chord** or **Thumb Brush** pattern.

After you have learned *The Midnight Special,* try using the **Alternate Bass Chord** or **Thumb Brush** pattern.

THE MIDNIGHT SPECIAL

Alternate BASS CHORD
(Thumb Brush)

Traditional

1. Get up ear - ly in the morn - in'___ hear the ding dong ring.

Hous - ton,___ you'd bet - ter walk right,

Go up to the ta - ble___ see the same old thing.

And you'd bet - ter not stag - ger___ and you'd bet - ter not fight.

Knife and fork are on the ta - ble,___ noth - in' in my pan,

The sher - iff will ar - rest you,___ judge will send you down,

had I com - plain'd a - bout it,___ I'm in trou - ble with the man.

you can bet your bot - tom dol - lar,___ You're pen - i - ten - ti'ry bound.

CHORUS

Let the mid - night spe - cial___ shine it's light on me,

Let the mid - night spec - ial___ shine it's ev - er lov-in' light on me.___

1.

2. If you ev - er go to ___

GO TELL AUNT RHODY

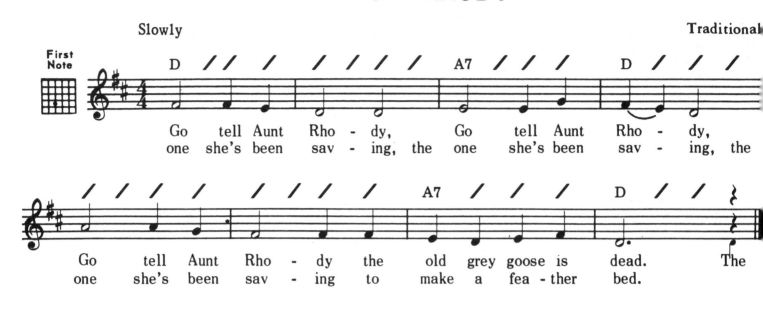

GOIN' DOWN THAT ROAD FEELIN' BAD

KEY OF A

Songs played or sung in the Key of A base their melody and chords on the A scale. The A chord now serves as "home base."

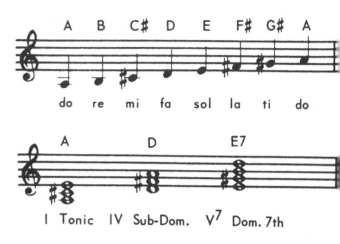

The PRIMARY chords in the Key of A are A, D and E7. They are constructed on the first, fourth and fifth tones of the A scale.

fig. 1 **Keyboard Analysis — A scale and primary chord**

A CHORD

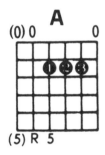

fig. 2 **Fretboard Analysis**

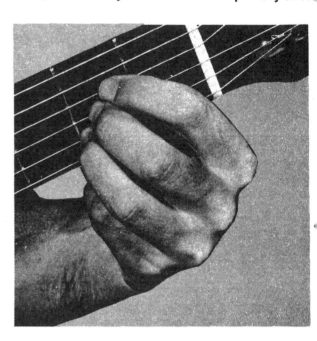

fig. 3 **A chord**

The A chord is the tonic or I chord in the Key of A. The Primary bass (R root) is located on the open 5th string. The Alternate bass (5 fifth) is located on either the 4th or 6th string.

OPTIONAL FINGERINGS

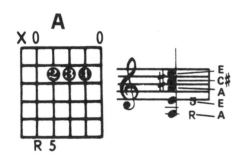

fig. 4 **This fingering requires the least amount of left hand movement when going to the E7 chord.**

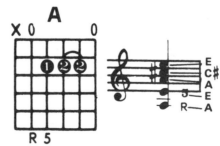

fig. 5 **Works best on guitars with narrow necks or with students who have large fingers.**

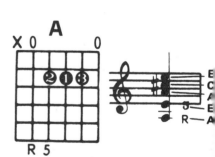

fig. 6 **This finger is related to the D7 finger — not particularly recommended by the author.**

E7 CHORD

E7

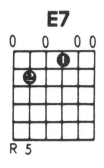

R 5

fig. 1 **Fretboard Analysis**

 THEORY

The E7 chord is the Dominant 7th in the Key of A. The Primary bass (R root) is located on the open 6th string. The 5th string, second fret is the Alternate bass (5 = fifth).

fig. 2 **E7 chord**

OPTIONAL FINGERINGS

E7

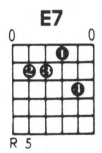

R 5

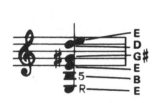

fig. 3 **This form of the E7 sounds "richer."**

E7

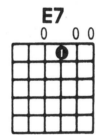

fig. 4 **Simplified version of the E7 chord.**

Using a down-stroke with a **Pick** or a **Brush** strum with the fingers, practice the following drills until you can make the change from the A to the E7 smoothly and without hesitation. Try using different fingerings. If you have control over the fourth finger of the left hand, I recommend using the optional A chord fingering (fig. 4 - preceding page) and the optional E7 chord fingering (fig. 3, - this page).

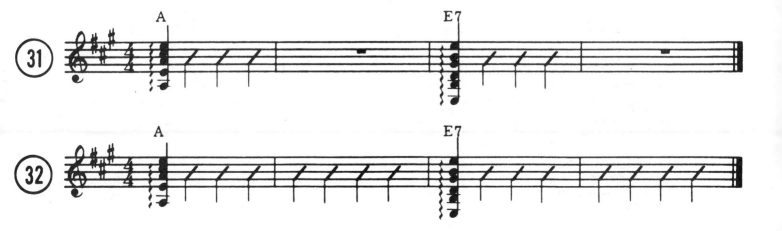

NINE POUND HAMMER

LONESOME VALLEY

JUST A CLOSER WALK WITH THEE

Slowly
Sacred

First Note

A
1. Just a clos-er walk with Thee,
2. I am weak and Thou art strong,
3. Thru this world of toil and snares,

Grant it Je-sus if you please.
Je-sus keep me from all wrong.
If I fal-ter, Lord who cares.

A7	D
Dai - ly walk-in' close to Thee.	Let it
I'll be sat-is-fied as long	As I
Who with me my bur-den shares?	None but

A	E7	A
be, dear Lord, let it be.		
walk let me walk, close to you.		
Thee, my dear Lord, none but Thee.		

Transpose *He's Got The Whole World, Irene, Give Me That Old Time Religion* and *Tom Dooley* into the key of A.

ALTERNATE BASS (Fifth)

In the case of the A chord, when performing the alternate bass pattern, the **fifth** (5) may be played on either the 4th or 6th string. When playing the E7 chord, alternate between the 6th string (R) and the 4th string (5).

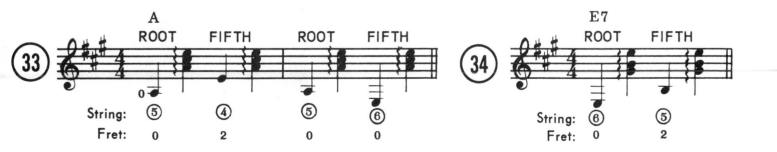

(33)
A
ROOT FIFTH ROOT FIFTH
String: ⑤ ④ ⑤ ⑥
Fret: 0 2 0 0

(34)
E7
ROOT FIFTH
String: ⑥ ⑤
Fret: 0 2

KEY OF E

fig. 1 **Keyboard Analysis — E scale and primary chords**

THEORY

The Primary chords in the Key of E are E, A and B7. They are built upon the first, fourth and fifth tones of the E scale.

E CHORD

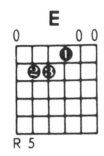

fig. 2 **Fretboard Analysis**

THEORY

In the Key of E, the E chord is the Tonic or I chord. The Primary bass (R) is located on the open 6th string. The Alternate bass (5) is located on the 5th string.

fig. 3 **E chord**

B7 CHORD

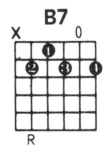

fig. 4 **Fretboard Analysis**

THEORY

The B7 chord functions as the Dominant 7th or V7 chord in the Key of E. The Primary bass (R) is located on the 5th string, second fret.

fig. 5 **B7 chord**

Using a **Pick** or a **Brush** strum, practice the following drill.

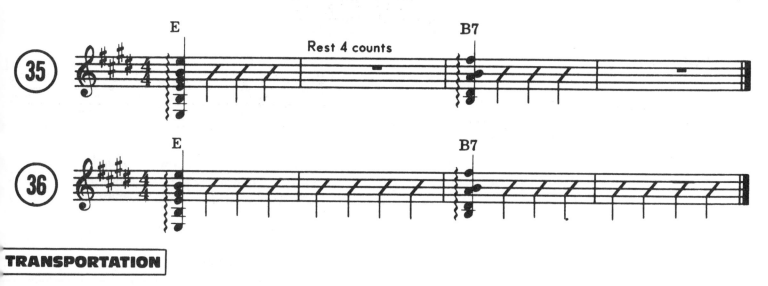

TRANSPORTATION

When progressing from the E to the B7 or from the B7 to the E, do not lift the second finger of the left hand. Let this finger serve as an anchor and guide.

For additional practice in using the D and B7 chords, transpose *Mary Ann, Good News* and *Puttin' On The Style* into the Key of E. Substitute the E and B7 chords for D and A7 chords.

ALTERNATE BASS (Fifth)

In the case of the B7 chord, in order to play the **Alternate Bass** (5) you must fret the 6th string at the second fret. Most guitarists lift the second finger of the left hand back and forth between the 5th and 6th string.

BASS CHORD (Thumb Brush) 3/4 * A

NOTE: Try using optional fingering.

BLUES STRUM

One characteristic of the blues type strum is the "shuffle" rhythm. This rhythm should be learned before attempting the strum. The **beat** is now divided into three parts. This rhythm pattern is called a **Triplet**. Tap the rhythm on your guitar.

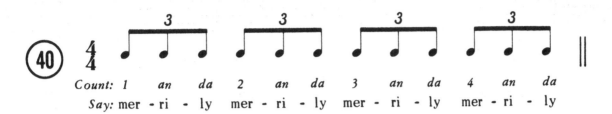

Now combine the time value of the first two notes of the triplet as indicated by the tie (‿) or the quarter note. fig. 1.

fig. 1 Two ways of writing the same rhythm.

On open strings and using a pick or a scratch strum, play the following drill. Once you have the rhythm, play the same drill while holding an E chord. ⊓ = down strum   V = up strum

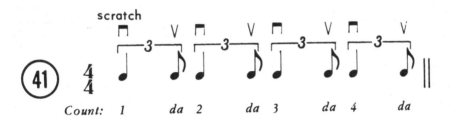

Now add the **Mute.** Muting is a right hand technique in which the strings are dampened (silenced) immediately following a down-stroke with the pick or a scratch with the index finger. It is done by rolling on to the **side** of the hand. This should be done with **one continuous** downward motion. On open strings, practice several **Mutes** in a row. Strive for a "chink" sound, **silence** between each mute and do not rush the beat.

Now practice the first part of the strum (1 da 2 — pause) on open strings or while holding an E chord. Then put it all together.

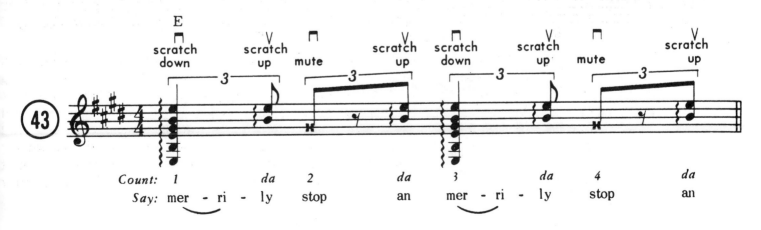

38

C.C. RIDER

TRANSPORTATION

* A7
02030

An alternate fingering should be used to eliminate unnecessary left hand movement.

CORNBREAD, PEAS AND BLACK MOLASSES

THE KEY OF Em

The melody and chords in the Key of Em are based on the Em scale. The Em chord assumes the role of "home base."

fig. 1 **Keyboard Analysis — Em scale and primary chords**

The primary chords in the Key of Em are Em, Am and B7. They are constructed on the first, fourth and fifth tones of the Em scale.

Em CHORD

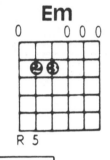

fig. 2 **Fretboard Analysis**

fig. 3 **Em chord**

THEORY

The Em chord is the Tonic or I chord. Its Primary bass (R) is located on the open 6th string. The Alternate Bass (5) is located on the 5th string, second fret.

Am CHORD

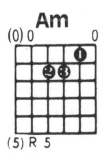

fig. 4 **Fretboard Analysis**

fig. 5 **Am chord**

THEORY

The Am chord is the Sub-Dominant or IV chord. The Primary bass (R) is the open 5th string. The Alternate Bass is either the open 6th string or the 4th string, second fret.

Using a pick or a brush strum, practice the following drill until you can make the changes smoothly and without hesitation. In going to the Em from the B7, do not lift the second finger of the left hand.

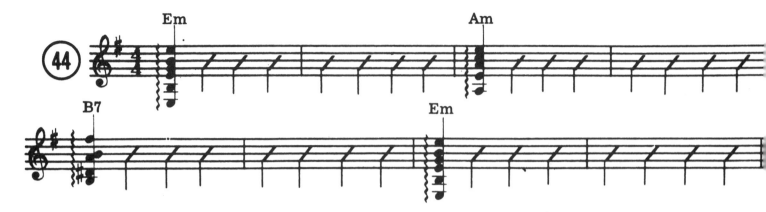

ALTERNATE BASS (Fifth)

Alternate the pick or thumb between the root (primary bass) and fifth (alternate bass) of the Em and Am chord.

THIS OLD HAMMER

Work Song adapted

SOMETIMES I FEEL LIKE A MOTHERLESS CHILD

Mournfully

Spiritual

LONESOME ROAD

BLUES STRUM

KEY OF C

In the Key of C, the C chord functions as the tonal center of "home base." The C scale serves as the skeleton upon which the melodies and harmonies are constructed.

The PRIMARY chords in the Key of C are C, F and G7. They are built upon the first, fourth and fifth tones of the C scale.

fig. 1 Keyboard Analysis - C scale and primary chords

G7 CHORD

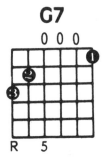

fig. 2 Fretboard Analysis

THEORY

The G7 chord is the Dominant 7th chord in the Key of C. The Primary bass (R) is located on the 6th string, third fret. The Alternate Bass is located on the open 4th string.

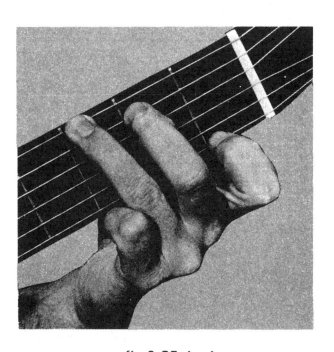

fig. 3 G7 chord

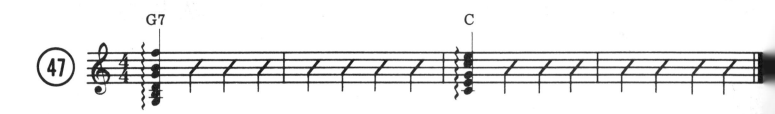

TRANSPORTATION

Notice the similarity between the G7 and C chord. The fingers of the left hand are in relatively the same position. Think of the G7 chord as an expanded C chord.

For additional practice using the C and G7 chords, transpose beginning songs played in the Key of D to the Key of C: *Some Folks Do, He's Got The Whole World, Good News* and *Rock-A My Soul.*

PAY ME MY MONEY DOWN

Traditional

I thought I heard the cap-tain say___ pay me___ my mon - ey down.___ To - mor - row is___ our sail - ing day.___

CHORUS

Pay me___ my mon - ey down.___ Pay me,___ oh, pay me,___ pay me___ my mon - ey down___

pay me___ or go to___ jail,___ pay me my mon - ey down.___

NOW THE DAY IS OVER

Joseph Barnby

Now the day is o - ver, Night is draw - ing___ nigh,___
When the morn-ing wak - ens, Then may I a - rise.___

Shad - ows of the eve - ning Steal a - cross the sky.
Pure and fresh and sin - less In Thy ho - ly eyes.

44

THUMB SWEEP

In the **Thumb Sweep,** the thumb (p) strums or sweeps downward (⊓) across the strings (low to high). The sweep most often begins with the root (R) of the chord. Keep the thumb rigid.

CALYPSO STRUM *

The **Calypso** strum uses a combination of the brush, sweep and scratch strums. **Brush** down across the strings on 1, **sweep** down across the strings on 1 *an*, **scratch** up on 2, **brush** down on 2 *an* (give emphasis), and then **scratch** up-down-up on *an 4 an*.

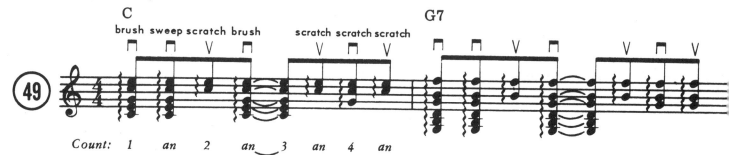

EVERYBODY LOVES SATURDAY NIGHT

* **Alternate CALYPSO SCRATCH strum:**

In the following **Calypso** strum, it is necessary to change to the A7 chord on the upbeat of 2 *an*. Apply this strum to *Banana Boat Song* contrasting it with a **Bass Down-Up** or **Thumb Scratch Alternating** (as indicated in the music).

BANANA BOAT SONG

Moderately

Island Folk Song

F CHORD

The F chord is more difficult to play than any of the previous chords because it requires the first finger of the left hand to cover (fret) more than one string. Guitarists and teachers approach the problem in a variety of ways and as a result there are many versions and fingerings of the F chord: three string version, four string version, five string version, six string version (with grand bar) and six string version (using the thumb). It is the author's intention to clarify the use of the various fingerings of the F chord.

SMALL BAR

When the first finger (index) is used to cover (fret) more than one string at a time it is called "barring." If two, three or four strings are fretted at the same time it is called the small or half bar. One version of the F chord is the small bar F chord.

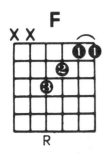

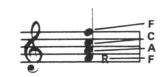

fig. 1 **Fretboard Analysis**

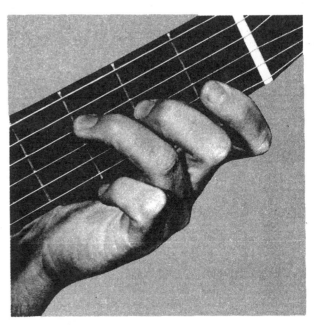

fig. 2 **F chord — small bar**

THEORY

The F chord is built on the fourth degree of the C scale and is the Sub-Dominant or IV chord. The Primary bass is located on the 4th string, third fret.

Begin by developing the ability to play a small bar (fig. 3). Since more pressure is necessary at the first fret, try and practice the small bar technique at the fifth and third frets. When you can successfully cover the 1st and 2nd strings with the index finger, progress on to steps 2 and 3.

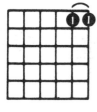

fig. 3 **Step one**

Index finger covers the 1st and 2nd strings. To avoid a "buzz," fret up close to the metal fret dividers. The pressure should be applied to the outer edge of the finger.

fig. 4 **Step two**

Now add the second finger to the chord. Avoid touching the string with the second finger. Fingernails must be short.

Step three is to add the third finger. Be careful not to touch the 3rd string with the third finger. fig. 2. Since the string "action" is generally higher at the first fret of the guitar, it is generally easier to develop the small bar technique on higher frets. Keep the wrist arched and the palm of the hand away from the neck of the guitar.

Another approach is to begin with a three string version of the F chord and eventually add the small bar.

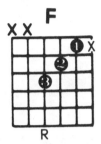

Note: The index finger deadens the 1st string (x) by lightly touching it with the inside of the finger. This simplified three string F chord should be eventually replaced with the small bar.

fig. 1 **F chord — three string**

ALTERNATE BASS

Two methods may be used to play the alternate bass (fifth of the chord) when using the small bar F chord.

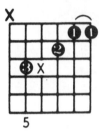

Move the third finger back and forth between the 4th and 5th string. This form leaves the fourth finger "free" for playing melody notes.

fig. 2

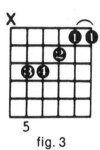

This five string version of the F chord allows you to play the alternate bass without moving the fingers.

fig. 3

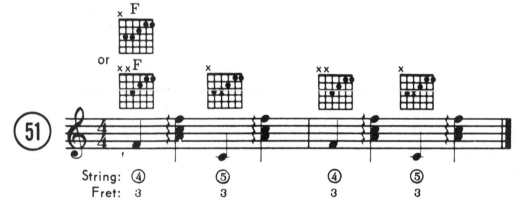

String:	④	⑤	④	⑤
Fret:	3	3	3	3

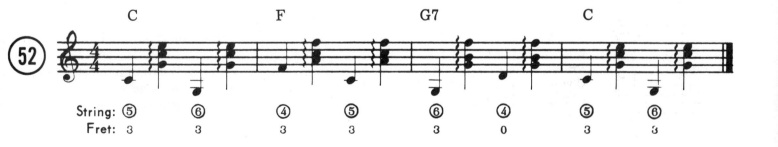

	C		F		G7		C	
String:	⑤	⑥	④	⑤	⑥	④	⑤	⑥
Fret:	3	3	3	3	3	0	3	3

TRANSPORTATION

When going from the C to the F chord, do not lift the second finger — simply roll the finger into the small bar position.

GRAND BAR

Unfortunately, the ability to play the small bar F chord does little to prepare you for the problems presented by the grand bar (full bar) F chord. The grand bar requires you to cover (fret) all six strings and often requires the use of the fourth finger to fret various strings.

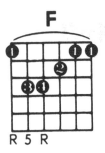

F

R 5 R

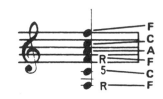

fig. 1 **Fretboard Analysis**

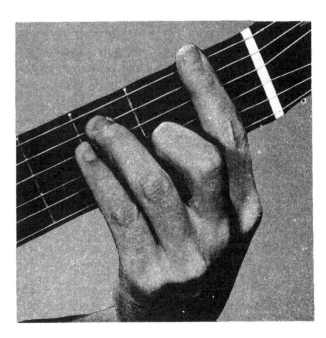

fig. 2 **F chord — grand bar**

THEORY

The Primary bass is located on either the 4th string, third fret or the 6th string, first fret. The Alternate bass is located on the 5th string, third fret.

Begin by developing the ability to play the grand bar (fig. 3). Because of the height of the strings at the first fret, it is recommended that you first apply the grand bar at the fifth fret and work your way down to the first fret. Secondly, add the second and third fingers to the grand bar (fig. 4). After you can play this chord (it is actually a dominant 7th chord), add the fourth finger – step three.

fig. 3 **Step one**

The index finger must be as straight as possible from the tip to the knuckle. The wrist is arched out with the thumb placed opposite the index finger (grip position). The palm of the hand must not touch the neck of the guitar.

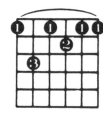

fig. 4 **Step two**

Now add the second and th[i] fingers to the chord. This is a[c] tually a dominant 7th form (F of the bar chord. The th[i] finger should not touch t[h] 4th string.

THE THUMB OPTION

In many styles of guitar, the use of the thumb to aid in fretting chords is frowned upon. There are some exceptions that are legitimate reasons for using the thumb. Some very involved jazz chords involve using the thumb and some country styles (finger-picking, ragtime, bluegrass) require the use of the thumb to fret chords in order to solve particular fingering problems. However, it is the author's opinion that the six string F chord (using the thumb) should not be used as a substitute for one's inability to play bar chords. It is presented so that you will understand its use. It is not recommended at this point.

Thumb ⟶

F

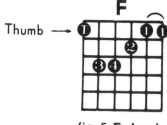

fig. 5 **F chord**

This form is most often used on a flat-top guitar that has a narrow neck. It is more difficult to play on a nylon string folk/classic guitar.

HARD, AIN'T IT HARD

Traditional

It's hard, ain't it hard, ain't it hard ___ to love one who nev-er__ will love you. ___ It's hard and it's hard, ain't it hard, great God, to love one who nev-er will be true. ___

JOHN HARDY

Bluegrass

Well now John Har-dy was a des-p'rate lit-tle man, he car-ried a ra-zor ev-'ry day, He killed a man on the West Vir-gin-ia line. You ought'a see John Har-dy get-tin' a-way, ought'a see John Har-dy get-ting a-way. ___

FREE STROKE (Fingers)

The index, middle and ring fingers of the right hand will now be used to play guitar accompaniments by plucking the string(s) together (simultaneously), individually (successively) or in a combination of the two.

Place the fingers on the strings as follows:

1.   index finger (*i* = indice) on the 3rd string (G)
2.   middle finger (*m* = medio) on the 2nd string (B)
3.   ring finger (*a* = anular) on the 1st string (E)

Bunch the fingers together with the tips touching the strings close to the fingernails. fig. 1 and 2.

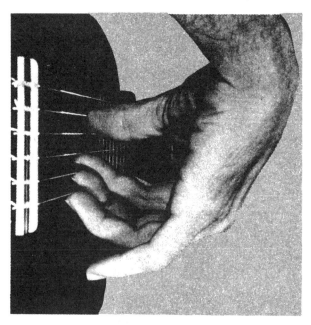

fig. 1 **Hand position — fingers curved**

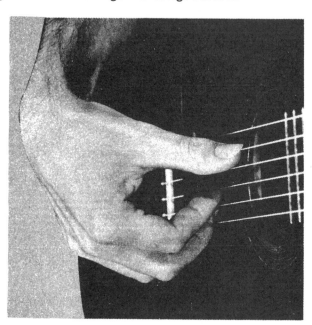

fig. 2 **Hand position — thumb extended**

In the **Free Stroke,** the fingers do not come to rest on the adjacent string. The finger(s) pluck the string(s) and pass over the neighboring (lower in pitch) string. The motion should be a "finger motion." Do not raise the hand. Simply curl the fingers into the hand. The forearm should still be positioned above the bridge bass. fig. 3 and 4.

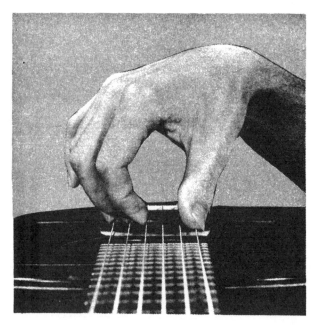

fig. 3 **Free stroke — preparation**

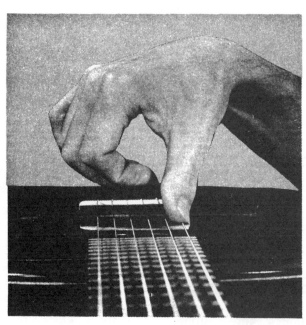

fig. 4 **Free stroke — completion**

ASS CHORD (Thumb Pluck) 3/4

the **Bass Chord 3/4,** pluck the root of the chord with a pick and strum the treble strings twice using a down-stroke. To orm the **Thumb Pluck 3/4,** the thumb (p) plucks the root of the chord (free stroke) and the fingers (i m a) pluck the le strings (3rd, 2nd and 1st) upward and inward simultaneously (free strokes).

STREETS OF LAREDO

As I _____ walked out in the streets of La - re - do, As

I _____ walked out in La - re - do one day, I

spied a young cow - boy wrapped up in white lin - en, Wrapped

up in white lin - en as cold as the clay.

The chords in parenthesis represent an alternate chord progression. It is not necessary to fret any strings in e Em chord. The F#m may be simplified by merely barring the second fret since the 4th and 5th strings are not lucked.

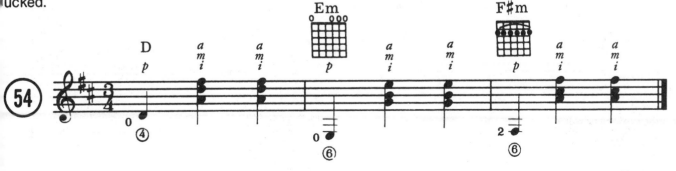

Apply the **Bass Chord** or the **Thumb Pluck** to *Beautiful Brown Eyes,* page 15.

BASS CHORD (Thumb Pluck) 4/4

In the pickstyle **Bass Chord 4/4** pattern, pluck the root of the chord on the first and third beats. Alternating to the fifth of the chord on the third beat is optional. Strum the chord on second and fourth beats. In the fingerstyle **Thumb Pluck 4/4** pattern, the thumb plucks the root of the chord and the fingers *(i m a)* pluck the 3rd, 2nd and 1st strings simultaneously.

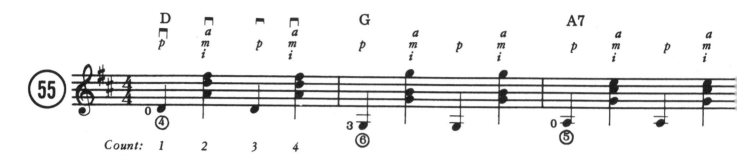

KUM BA YAH

Apply the **Bass Chord** or the **Thumb Pluck** to *Banks Of The Ohio*, page 17. Add to the accompaniment by **alternating** the bass.

BROKEN CHORD (Plucking Arpeggio) 3/4

When parts of a chord are played on various beats in a measure, it is called a "broken" chord or an arpeggio. In pickstyle, use a succession of down-strokes (⊓) to play a slow **Broken Chord 3/4** pattern. In the **Plucking Arpeggio 3/4**, the thumb *(p)* plucks the root of the chord, the index *(i)* finger plucks the 3rd string and the middle and ring fingers *(m a)* pluck the 2nd and 1st strings simultaneously. Some country, rock and blues players use a **combination** of the **pick** and the **middle** *(m)* and **ring** *(a)* fingers to play arpeggios. The pick plucks the notes on the 6th through 3rd strings and the middle and ring fingers pluck the 2nd and 1st strings.

SILENT NIGHT

BROKEN CHORD (Plucking Arpeggio)

Traditional

1. Si - lent night, ho - ly night, All is calm, all is bright. Round yon vir - gin Moth - er and child. Ho - ly In - fant so ten - der and mild. Sleep in heav - en - ly peace. Sleep in hea - ven - ly peace.

2. Si - lent night, ho - ly night, Shep - herds quake, at the sight. Glor - ies stream from heav - en a - far. Heav'n - ly host sing hal - le - lu - jah. Christ the Sav - ior is born. Christ the Sav - ior is born.

The Broken Chord or **Plucking Arpeggio** works well with *Amazing Grace*, page 36. The bass could **alternate** back and forth between the fifth of the chord.

54

BROKEN CHORD (Plucking Arpeggio) 4/4

Use all down-strokes to play the pickstyle **Broken Chord 4/4** pattern. As an option, try using an up pick (⋁) for all notes played on the 3rd string. In the fingerstyle **Plucking Arpeggio 4/4** pattern, the thumb plucks the root of the chord and can alternate to the fifth on the third beat. The index *(i)* finger plucks the 3rd string. The middle *(m)* and ring *(a)* fingers pluck the 2nd and 1st strings together. Give emphasis (stress) to the first and third beats of the measure. Try the **combination** pick and fingers technique. Pluck the 2nd and 1st strings with the middle and ring fingers. Pluck all other notes in the chord with the pick.

BROKEN CHORD
(Plucking Arpeggio)

CHILDREN, GO WHERE I SEND THEE

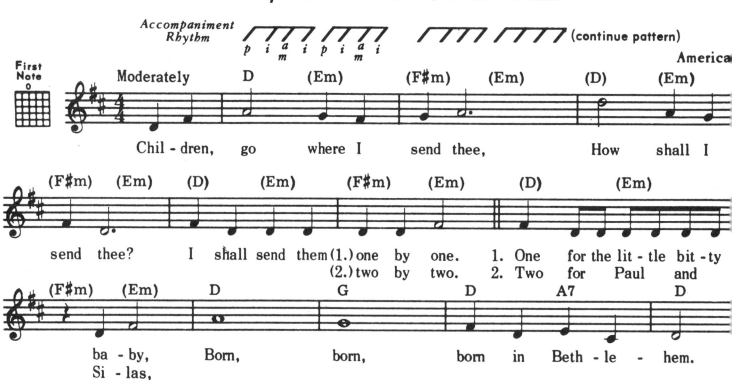

Try this alternate chord progression (chords in parentheses). It is not necessary to fret any strings on the Em chord and the F#m can be simplified by merely barring the second fret.

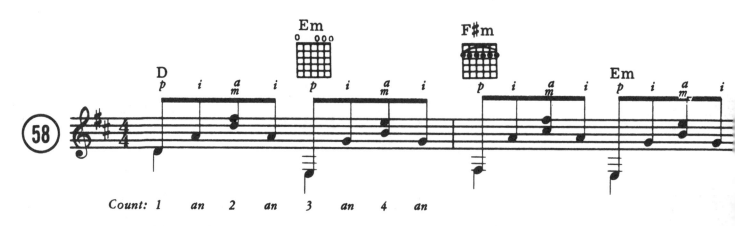

Try using the Broken Chord or **Plucking Arpeggio** with *Just A Closer Walk With Thee* on page 33 and *Now The Day Is Over* on page 43.

AURA LEE

BROKEN CHORD
(Plucking Arpeggio)
alternating bass - optional

ALL THROUGH THE NIGHT

PLUCKING ARPEGGIO

BROKEN CHORD (Arpeggio) 3/4

In the **Broken Chord** or **Arpeggio,** each tone in the chord is plucked individually. In pickstyle, a **sweep** technique can be used to play the broken chord pattern. When you have two or more consecutive notes on adjacent strings, it takes less motion to play them with one pick direction. Practice the picking pattern indicated below (four down-strokes and two up-strokes). In fingerstyle, the thumb *(p)* plucks the root of the chord, the index *(i)* finger plucks the 3rd string, the middle *(m)* finger plucks the 2nd string and the ring *(a)* finger plucks the 1st string.

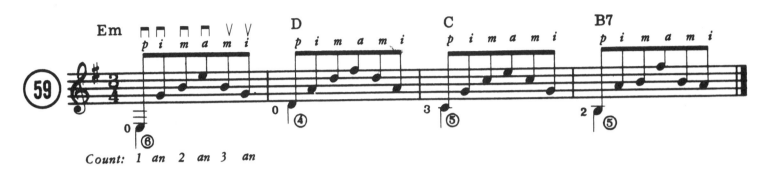

Count: 1 an 2 an 3 an

GREENSLEEVES
(What Child Is This)

English

BROKEN CHORD (Arpeggio) 4/4

In pickstyle, use alternating down and up-strokes with a pick or use the *sweep* pick (two consecutive down-strokes) going from the 3rd to the 2nd string on *an* 2. In fingerstyle, the thumb *(p)* plucks the root of the chord, the index *(i)* finger plucks the 3rd string, the middle *(m)* finger plucks the 1st string.

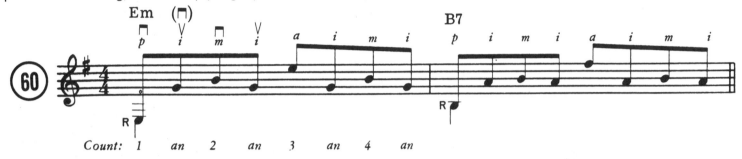

JOSHUA FIT THE BATTLE OF JERICHO

Josh-ua fit the bat-tle of Jer - i- cho,__ Jer - i-cho,__ Jer - i-cho,__

Josh-ua fit the bat-tle of Jer - i - cho__ And the walls came tum-bl - in' down. You may

talk a-bout your King of Gi - de - on, You may talk a - bout your men of Saul. But there

none like good old Josh - ua, At the bat-tle of Jer - i - cho.

CRUEL WAR

BROKEN CHORD
(Arpeggio)

Traditional

1. The cruel war is rag - ing, John - ny has to
2. To - mor - row is Sun - day, Mon - day is the

fight; I _____ want to be with him from morn - ing 'til night.
day, that your cap - tain will call you, And you must o - bey.

PINCH TECHNIQUE

When the pick (or thumb) and **one** finger are plucked together (simultaneously), it is called a **Pinch.** In pickstyle, use down-strokes and a combination of the pick and either the middle *(m)* or ring *(a)* finger to perform the pinch technique. On the third and fourth beats of exercise 61, the middle or ring finger plucks the 1st string in combination with a down-stroke of the pick. In fingerstyle, the ring *(a)* finger pinches in combination with the thumb *(p)*.

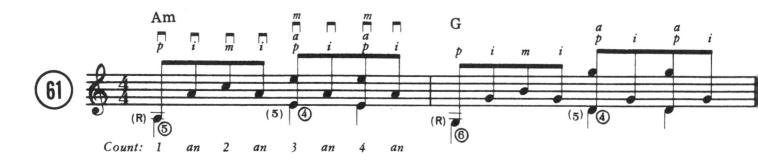

WHAT SHALL WE DO WITH A DRUNKEN SAILOR?

Traditional

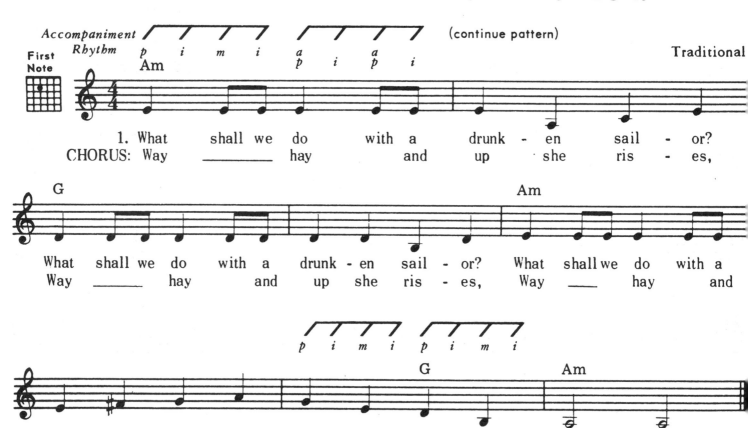

1. What shall we do with a drunk - en sail - or?
CHORUS: Way _____ hay and up she ris - es,

What shall we do with a drunk - en sail - or? What shall we do with a
Way _____ hay and up she ris - es, Way ___ hay and

drunk - en sail - or, ear - lye in the morn - ing?
up she ris - es ear - lye in the morn - ing.

The following are other **pinch** patterns that may be applied to familiar songs.

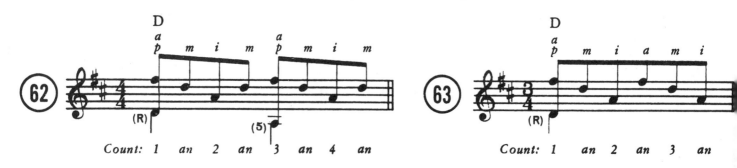

CALYPSO

In Pickstyle, use a *sweep* on the first 4 notes (consecutive down-strokes) and then alternate the pick on beats *an* 4 *an*. Accent (>) or give emphasis to the 1st string. In fingerstyle, work out of the basic **classical** guitar hand position. The thumb *(p)* plucks the root (R) of the chord of the chord, the index *(i)*, middle *(m)* and ring *(a)* fingers pluck the 3rd, 2nd and st strings.

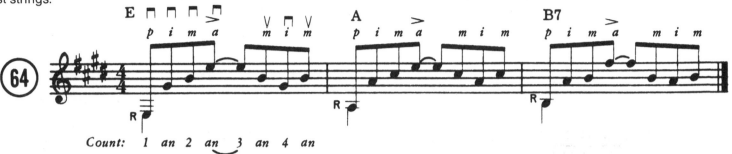

SLOOP JOHN B

In the following fingerstyle variation, accents (>) are very important. It will help to think of the rhythm pattern as

FINGER-PICKING

Finger-picking is an instrumental style of playing the guitar that was developed by black southern American musicians around the turn of the century. Early innovators of this style include Mississippi John Hurt, Blind Blake, Robert Johnson, Mance Lipscomb and Rev. Gary Davis. This style is reminiscent of the *piano swing-bass* and *ragtime* styles of playing. On the guitar, the right hand thumb plays a rhythmic bass on the lower sounding strings while the fingers pick out the melody on the treble strings. This produces a sound similar to the pianist playing a "boom-chuck" pattern with the left hand while the right hand plays the melody.

One of the most notable and influencial finger-picking guitarists is Merle Travis. He developed a right hand fingerstyle approach to playing the guitar that became so identified with him that it bears his name - "travis picking." Country pickin', travis pickin', two finger pickin', three finger pickin', pattern pickin' and just plain pickin' are various names given to this guitar style. The two most distinguishing characteristics are:

1. The **steady beat established by the thumb** or **pick** playing on every **down beat (1 2 3 4)**.
2. **The syncopated** patterns produced by the fingers plucking the treble strings on the **up beats** (1 *an* 2 *an* 3 *an* 4 *an*)

PICKSTYLE

As the name suggests, finger-picking is essentially a fingerstyle technique. Pickstyle players, however, can assimilate this style by using a **combination** of pick and fingerstyle techniques. When playing finger-picking patterns, use the pick to pluck the 6th, 5th, 4th and 3rd strings. Use the middle *(m)* finger to pluck the 2nd string and the ring *(a)* finger to pluck the 1st string. Use the pinch technique to simultaneously play the bass and treble strings. Let the notes in the chords ring throughout the measure.

FINGERSTYLE

In the finger-picking style, the **thumb** *(p)* is required to play (pluck) on every downbeat. To achieve the necessary speed and to avoid interference with the fingers, use a **free stroke** with the thumb - see page 10. In the free stroke, the thumb does not come to rest on the adjacent (higher in pitch) string. Also, use free strokes with the **index** *(i)* and **middle** *(m)* fingers - see page 50.

The fingers of the right hand are placed as follows:

1. the **index** *(i)* finger is placed on 2nd string (B).
2. The **middle** *(m)* finger is placed on the 1st string (E).

The **thumb** *(p)* continues to oppose the fingers. Keep the thumb rigid, straight and extended. Do not allow the first joint of the thumb to collapse toward the fingers, fig. 1.

Pickstyle: While holding the D chord begin to "groove" the pick pattern - Ex. 66. The pick plucks on every **downbeat** and alternates between the root of the chord and the third string. In Ex. 67, the middle *(m)* finger plucks the 2nd string and in Ex. 68 the ring *(a)* finger is used to pluck the 1st string.

Fingerstyle: The thumb *(p)* plucks (free stroke) on every **downbeat** and alternates between the root of the chord (4th string) and the 3rd string - Ex. 66. In Ex. 67 and 68, the index *(i)* and the middle *(m)* fingers are added to the pattern. It is important to accent (>) or stress certain tones plucked with the fingers.

Apply the finger-picking pattern introduced in Ex. 68 to *Reuben's Train*.

REUBEN'S TRAIN

FINGER–PICKING

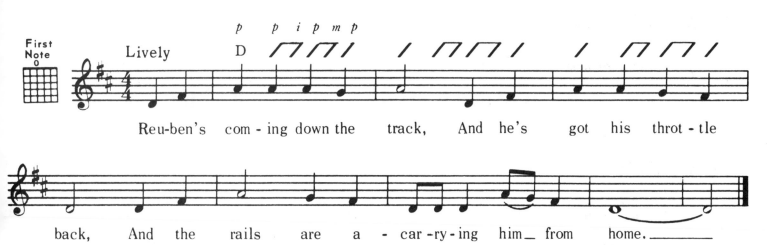

Reu-ben's com-ing down the track, And he's got his throt-tle back, And the rails are a-car-ry-ing him from home.

The pick and thumb pattern remains the same on all chords: root - 3rd string - root - 3rd string. On the C chord, the pick or thumb alternates between the 5th string (root) and the 3rd string.

LITTLE MAGGIE

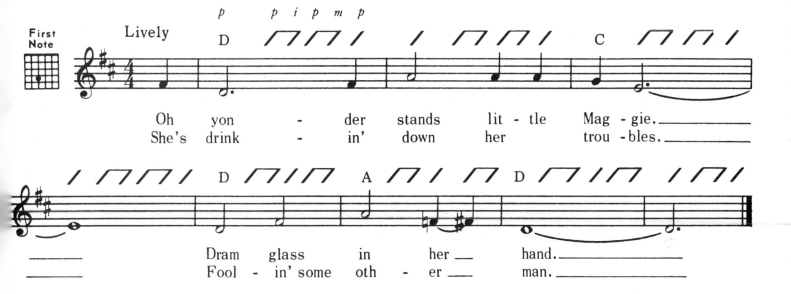

Oh yon - der stands lit-tle Mag-gie.
She's drink - in' down her trou-bles.

Dram glass in her hand.
Fool - in' some oth - er man.

ALTERNATE BASS

In the **Alternate Bass** pattern, the pick or thumb *(p)* plucks the fifth (5) of the chord on the third downbeat of the measure. Continue to pluck the 3rd string on the second and fourth downbeats of the measure. This pattern remains the same regardless of the chord.

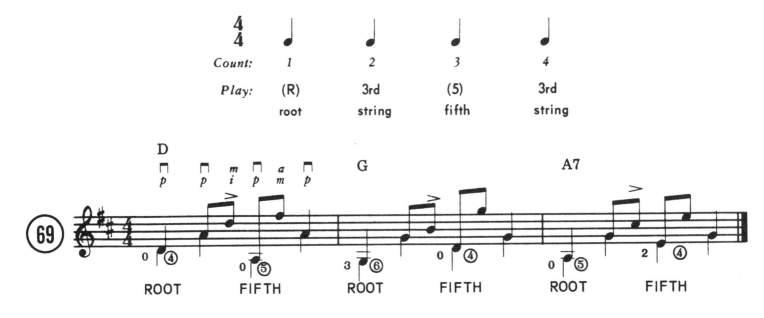

Count:	1	2	3	4
Play:	(R)	3rd	(5)	3rd
	root	string	fifth	string

WHEN THE SAINTS GO MARCHING IN

Oh when the saints _____ go march-ing in _____
Oh when the sun _____ be - gins to shine, _____

_____ Oh when the saints go march - ing in. _____ How I
_____ Oh when the sun be - gins to shine. _____ How I

want to be in that num - ber, _____ when the
want to be in that num - ber, _____ when the

saints go march - ing in. _____
saints go march - ing in. _____

OTHER PATTERNS

The pick or thumb *(p)* continues the same pattern but the finger pattern is changed in the following finger-picking patterns. Alternating to the fifth (5) of the chord is optional.

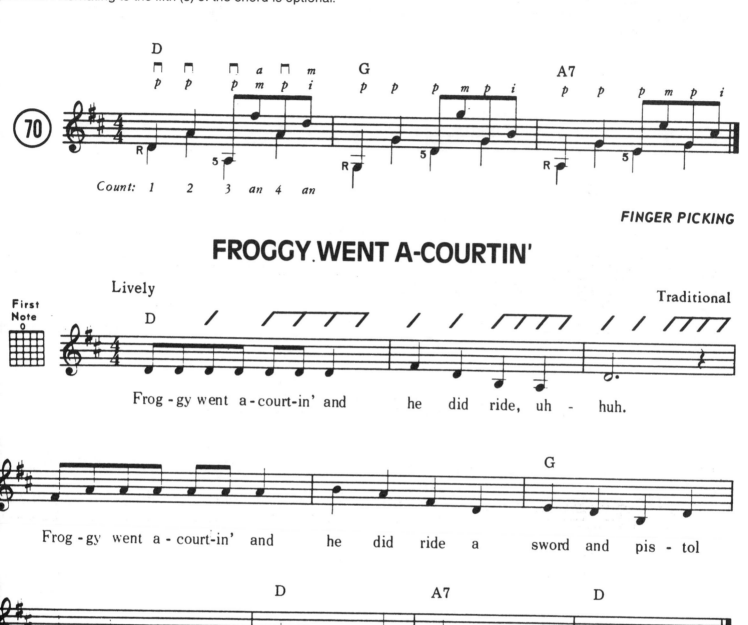

FINGER PICKING

FROGGY WENT A-COURTIN'

Lively   Traditional

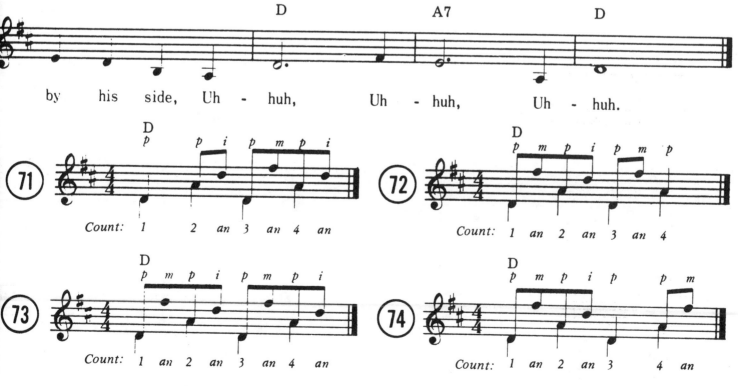

PINCH PATTERNS

In pickstyle, it is called a **pinch** when the pick and the middle *(m)* finger or the pick and the ring *(a)* finger pluck the bass and treble strings together. When the thumb *(p) and index (i)* finger or the thumb *(p)* and middle *(m)* finger pluck the bass the treble strings together, it is call a **pinch** in fingerstyle.

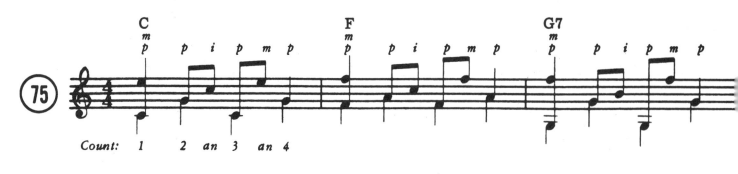

RAILROAD BILL

Rail - road   Bill,   Rail - road   Bill,
Rail - road   Bill,   took   me   a - long

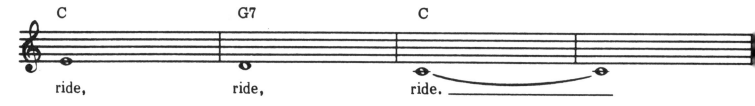

He nev - er   worked   and ___   he nev - er   will,   Gon - na
Taught me this   cho - rus ___   taught me this   song,

ride,   ride,   ride. _____

Try applying the following **pinch** patterns to songs you know. Alternate the pick or the thumb to the fifth (5) on the third beat when you have the patterns "grooved."

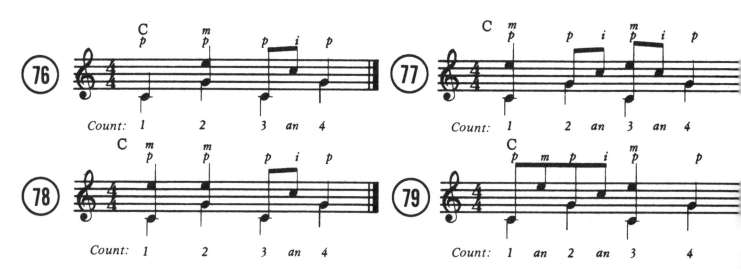

Try various **finger-picking** patterns with the following songs. The goal is to eventually "break out" of patterns and to use more than one accompaniment rhythm. Try mixing it up a little. Develop new patterns.

MICHAEL, ROW THE BOAT ASHORE

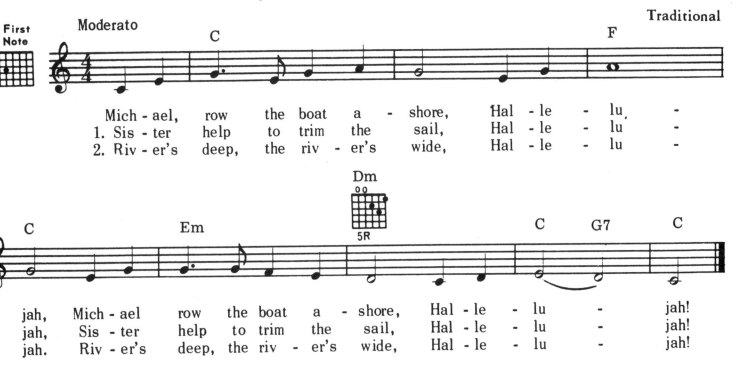

Mich - ael, row the boat a - shore, Hal - le - lu -
1. Sis - ter help to trim the sail, Hal - le - lu -
2. Riv - er's deep, the riv - er's wide, Hal - le - lu -

jah, Mich - ael row the boat a - shore, Hal - le - lu - jah!
jah, Sis - ter help to trim the sail, Hal - le - lu - jah!
jah. Riv - er's deep, the riv - er's wide, Hal - le - lu - jah!

EVERY NIGHT WHEN THE SUN GOES DOWN

CHORUS: Ev - 'ry night _____ when the sun goes down _____ Ev - 'ry night _
1. love don't weep _____ true love don't mourn, _True love, don't weep_

_____ when the sun goes down. _____ Ev - 'ry night _____ when the sun goes
_____ true love don't mourn. _____True love don't weep_____ true love don't

down. _____ I hang my head _____ and mourn - ful cry. _____1. True
mourn. _____ I goin' a - way _____ to Mar - ble - town. _____

Section Two: NOTATION

This section includes *theory, musical notation, songs and ensembles* arranged for the guitar. The material in the **Notation** section should be studied along with and in conjunction with the *chords, theory, strums* and *songs presented on pages 6-65.*

Either **pickstyle** or **fingerstyle** (plectrum) right hand techniques may be applied in the **Notation** section. In the pickstyle, a pick (plectrum) is used to pluck or stroke the strings. In fingerstyle, the index *(i)* and middle *(m)* fingers will *generally* pluck the treble strings and the thumb *(p)* will pluck the bass strings.

PICKSTYLE

The **pick** (flat-pick, plectrum) is held between the thumb and index finger of the right hand, fig. 1.

1. Bend the **index** finger toward the thumb.
2. Place the **thumb** on the side of the index finger along the first joint.
3. Insert the **pick** between the thumb and the index finger so that a triangle is exposed.

A variety of pick sizes and thickness (gauges) are available. Review page 5.

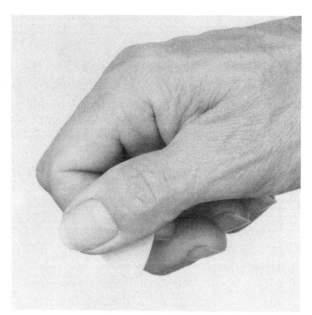

Fig. 1 **Pick position**

The **down stroke** (⊓) is the basic stroke. When stroking the strings, do not allow the right hand thumb to collapse. Use a wrist motion and keep the thumb rigid. The middle, ring and little fingers on the right hand lightly touch the guitar (on the pick guard) and move with the hand. The author does not recommend anchoring any portion of the right hand to the guitar. When plucking all but the 1st string, allow the pick to come to rest against the next (higher in pitch) string and then return the pick to its beginning position. In speed picking, stop the pick short of the next string.

In general, the **up-stroke** (V) is used to play notes that occur on up-beats *(an)* as in playing eighth notes. In playing the up-stroke, follow through only enough to finish picking the string and immediately return to the starting point. Use a minimum amount of motion.

Use **alternate** down-strokes and up-strokes (⊓ V) to play successive eighth or sixteenth notes. Use an economy of motion. Stop short of the adjacent strings when picking alternating down and up-strokes.

FINGERSTYLE

REST STROKE (Fingers). Alternate the index *(i)* and middle *(m)* fingers using a **rest stroke** when playing successive single notes or melodies. Perform the **rest stroke** by plucking (pressing) the string and coming to rest on the next (lower in pitch) string. The motion for the rest stroke comes from the third joint (where the finger joins the hand). Do not allow the finger to collapse at the second joint.

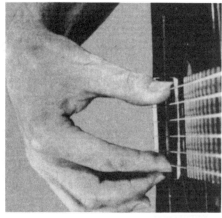

fig. 2 **Preparation - index finger**

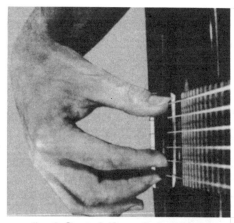

fig. 3 **Completion - index finger**

REST STROKE (Thumb). Pluck the 4th string with the **thumb** and come to rest on the 3rd string. The 3rd string is used to "brake" the thumb's downward motion, fig 1 and 2. Keep the thumb rigid. The motion of the rest stroke comes from the joint where the thumb joins the hand. Do not bend the thumb at the first joint.

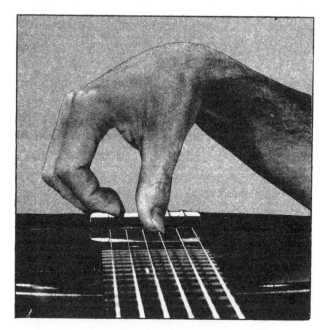

fig.1 **Preparation - thumb**

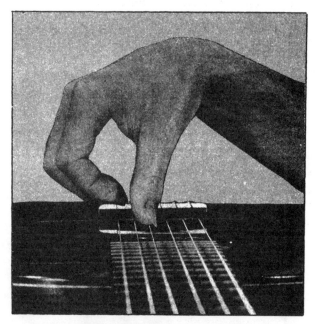

fig. 2 **Completion - thumb**

Rest strokes are used to play single note lead lines and melodies. Learn to alternate the **index** *(i)* and **middle** *(m)* fingers. In general, when you are working out alternating patterns *(i m* or *m i),* try to use the middle finger when moving to higher sounding strings and the index finger when moving to lower in pitch strings. the index and middle fingers can be used to play rest strokes on the treble and bass strings. The rest stroke with the **thumb** *(p)* is generally used on the bass strings (6th, 5th and 4th strings) and needs to be executed from the same hand position as used to perform the free stroke.

EXPLANATION OF SYMBOLS

In the fingerstyle technique - **p, i, m, a** - placed above the note indicate which finger of the **right** hand to use to pluck the note.

  p = thumb (pulgar)   ***m*** = middle (medio)
  i = index (indice)   ***a*** = ring (anular)

Circled numbers ①②③④⑤⑥ placed below the note indicate the string upon which to play.

The numbers 1, 2, 3, and 4 placed next to a note indicate **left** hand fingering. A zero (0) stands for an **open** string.

In pickstyle, (⊓) indicates a **down-stroke** and (V) indicates an up-stroke.

The notes are placed on the **staff** which consists of 5 lines and 4 spaces. The first seven letters of the alphabet are used to name the notes: **A B C D E F G**

  The **treble** or **G clef** placed on the staff designates the second line as G.

Remember that the guitar is a **transposing instrument.** Notes **written** on the staff **sound** an octave (eight notes) lower.

fig. 3 **Finger-style symbols, string and left hand fingerings**

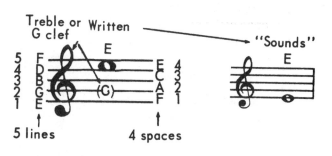

fig. 4 **Notation signs and symbols**

WHOLE NOTE

In most music the Whole Note receives 4 beats or counts.

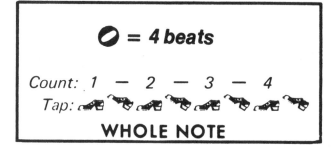

$\oslash$ = **4 beats**

Count: 1 — 2 — 3 — 4
Tap:

WHOLE NOTE

FIRST NOTE — G

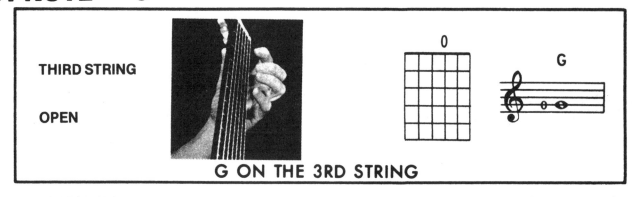

THIRD STRING

OPEN

G ON THE 3RD STRING

1

Count: 1 — 2 — 3 — 4

HALF NOTE

The Half Note receives two beats or two counts. It has only half as much time value as the Whole Note.

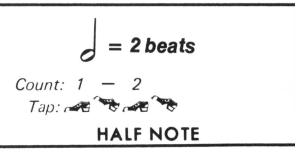

$\downarrow$ = **2 beats**

Count: 1 — 2
Tap:

HALF NOTE

2

Count: 1 — 2   3 — 4   1 — 2 — 3 — 4

NEW NOTE — A

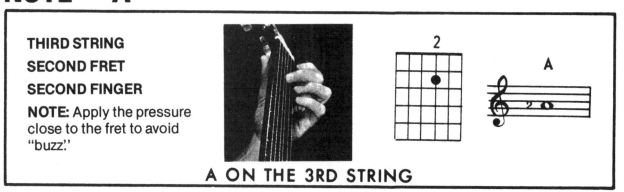

THIRD STRING

SECOND FRET

SECOND FINGER

NOTE: Apply the pressure close to the fret to avoid "buzz."

A ON THE 3RD STRING

*Chord symbols for teacher accompaniment or divide the class into four groups.

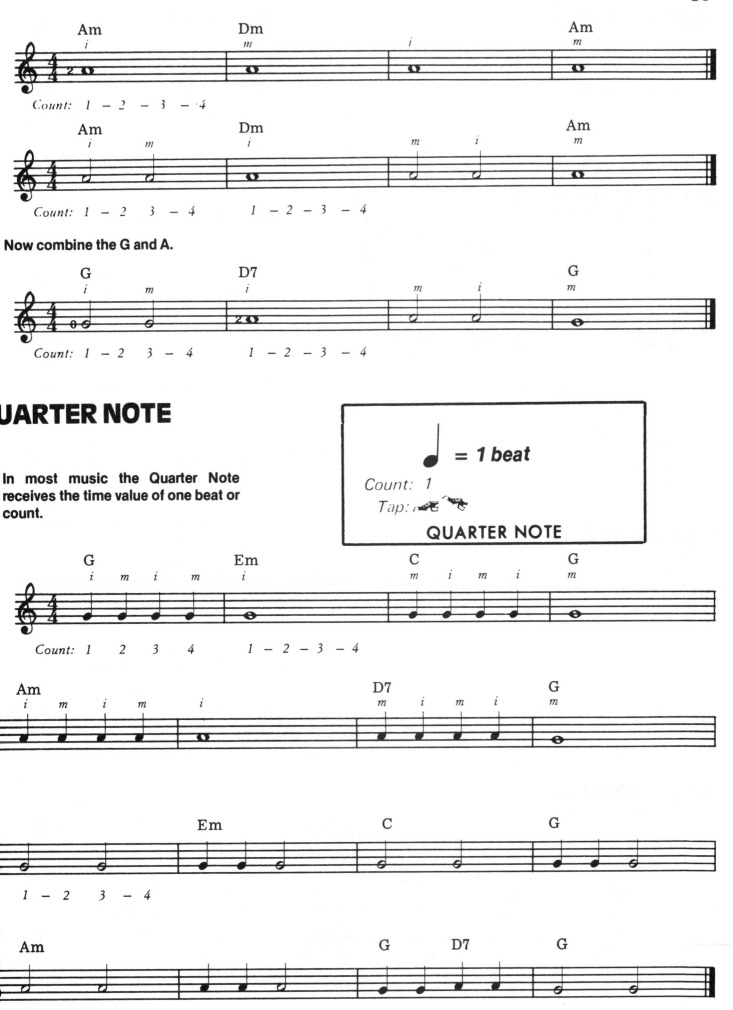

Now combine the G and A.

QUARTER NOTE

In most music the Quarter Note receives the time value of one beat or count.

♩ = *1 beat*

Count: *1*
Tap:

QUARTER NOTE

NEW NOTE — B

SECOND STRING

OPEN

0

B

B ON THE 2ND STRING

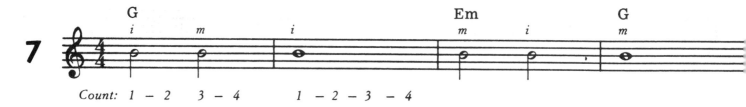

7

Count: 1 – 2   3 – 4   1 – 2 – 3 – 4

Review of the G, A and B. Circled number ③ indicates string.

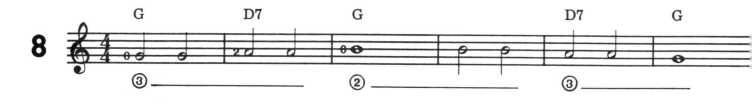

8

③ _____   ② _____   ③ _____

9

Count: 1   2   3 – 4

AT PIERROT'S DOOR

Moderate

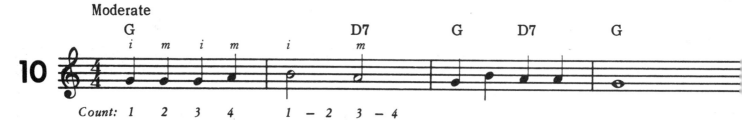

10

Count: 1   2   3   4   1 – 2   3 – 4

NEW NOTE — C

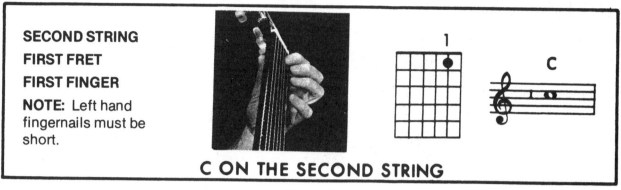

SECOND STRING
FIRST FRET
FIRST FINGER

NOTE: Left hand fingernails must be short.

C ON THE SECOND STRING

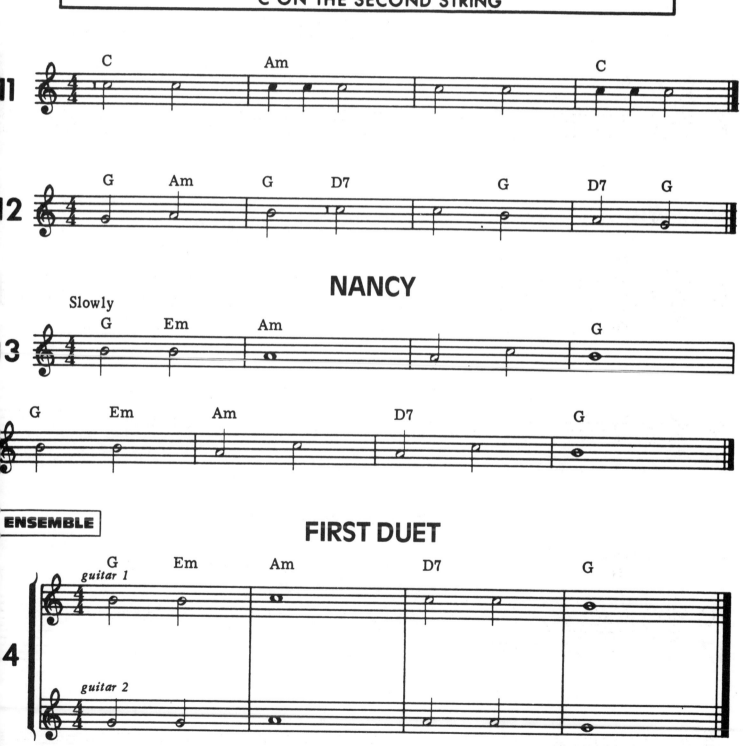

NANCY

FIRST DUET

Optional: Add chord accompaniment to Study No. 14.

DOTTED HALF NOTE

A dot may be added to any note. The dot adds time value to the note equal to one-half the note's time value.

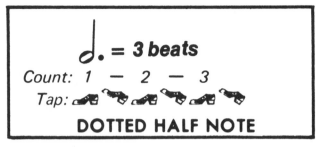

𝅗𝅥. = 3 beats

Count: 1 — 2 — 3

Tap:

DOTTED HALF NOTE

15 Em   Am   B7   Em

Count: 1 — 2 — 3   4

3/4 TIME

Beats are grouped together to form measures. Measures are divided by Bar Lines. The time signature tells how many beats are in each measure.

3 = 3 beats in each measure

4 = quarter note gets one beat

3/4 TIME SIGNATURE

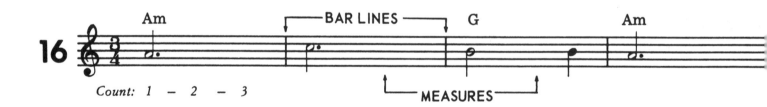

16 Am   — BAR LINES —   G   Am

Count: 1 — 2 — 3

— MEASURES —

WENDY'S MOOD

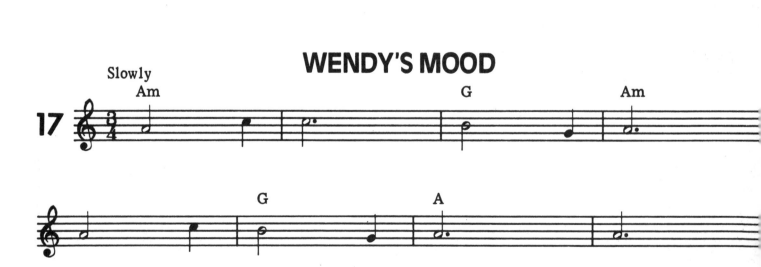

Slowly
Am   G   Am

17

G   A

74

ODE TO JOY
(Theme from Symphony No. 9)

Ludwig Van Beethoven

AURA LEE

Traditional

EIGHTH NOTES

The basic beat or count may be divided into two parts — a down-beat and an up-beat. Two eighth notes equal a quarter note.

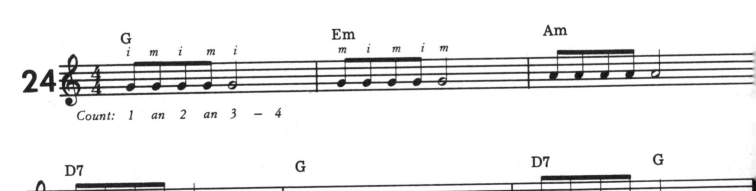

Count: 1 an 2 an 3 — 4

2/4 TIME

In 2/4 Time the beats or counts are grouped in two's. Two beats to a measure.

> **2** = 2 beats in each measure
>
> **4** = quarter note gets one beat
>
> **2/4 TIME SIGNATURE**

A CHRISTMAS SONG

REPEAT SIGN(S)

Repeat signs consist of two dots placed before or after a double bar. Repeat the music enclosed within the signs.

> **Repeat to here** ← ... → **Double Bar**
>
> **REPEAT SIGNS**

ENSEMBLE

LITTLE BIRD

Traditional

Study No. 26 may be combined with Study No. 56 (Bass Part).

NEW NOTE — E

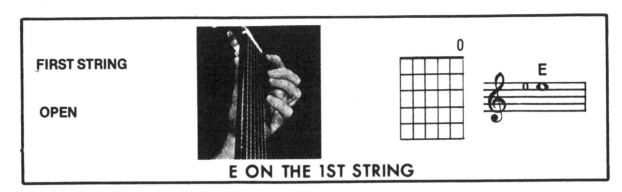

FIRST STRING

OPEN

E ON THE 1ST STRING

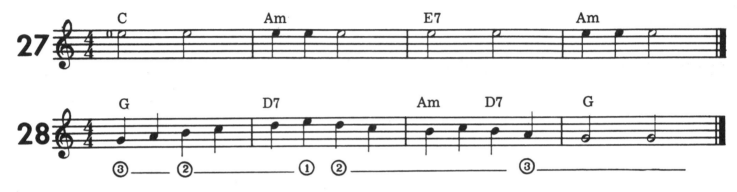

27

28

ENSEMBLE

AT PIERROT'S DOOR (Duet)

Moderate

Traditional

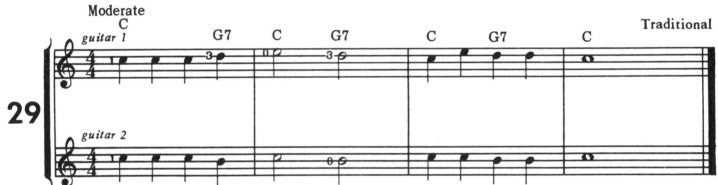

29

LONG, LONG AGO

Moderate   Traditional

30

ENSEMBLE

NED'S BLUES

Study No. 31 may be combined with Study No. 48.

DOTTED QUARTER NOTE

A dot added to a quarter note adds ½ beat (one-half the time value of a quarter) to the note.

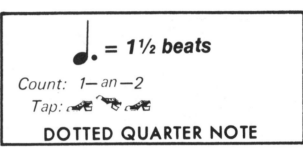

$\downarrow. = 1½$ beats

Count: 1— an —2
Tap:

DOTTED QUARTER NOTE

Count: 1 — 2 an 3   4

MICHAEL, ROW THE BOAT ASHORE

Traditional

Count: 3   4   1 — 2 an 3   4

ALL THROUGH THE NIGHT

Traditional

Count: 1 — 2 an 3   4

TIE

The time value of one note may be added to another with the use of the Tie. Curved lines (‿ or ⌢) "Tie" the time value of two or more notes together.

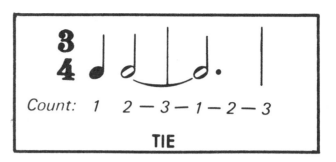

BEAUTIFUL BROWN EYES

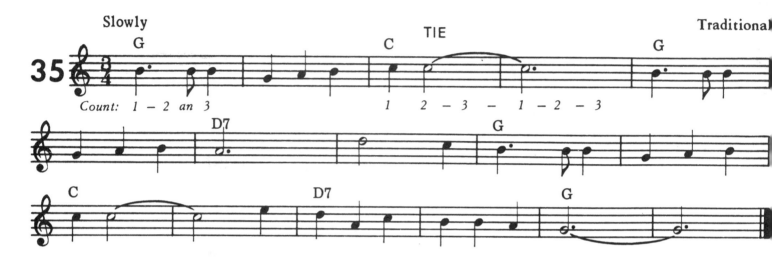

NEW NOTE — F

FIRST STRING

FIRST FRET

FIRST FINGER

F ON THE 1ST STRING

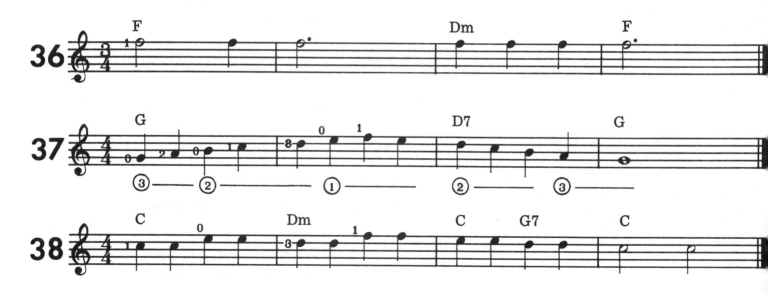

PLAISIR D' AMOUR
(The Joy Of Love)

Waltz Tempo

Martini

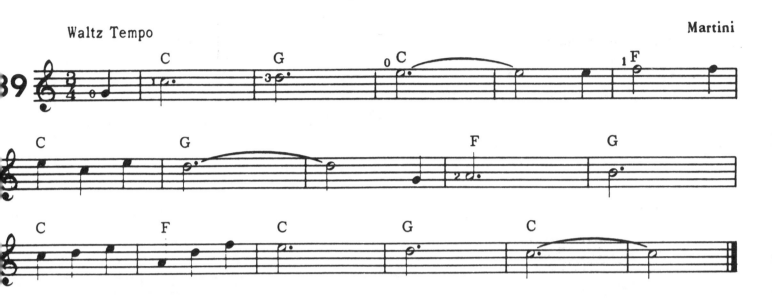

QUARTER REST

For each type of note, there is a rest with the same name and time value. This is a symbol indicating silence.

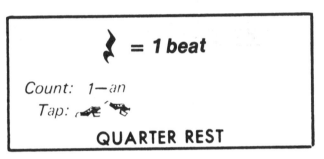

$\large\xi$ = **1 beat**

Count: 1—an
Tap:

QUARTER REST

ENSEMBLE

SYMPHONY NO. 1
(Theme, Fourth Movement)

Johannes Brahms

Slowly

f **Dynamic Sign**

Combine Study No. 40 with Study No. 66 (Bass).

DYNAMIC SIGNS

Signs of musical expression. Dynamic signs tell how to interpret the music as to softness and loudness.

p	=	*piano* (soft)
mp	=	*mezzo piano* (medium soft)
m	=	*mezzo* (medium)
mf	=	*mezzo forte* (medium loud)
f	=	*forte* (loud)

DYNAMIC SIGNS

NEW NOTE — G

FIRST STRING

THIRD FRET

THIRD FINGER

NOTE: Keep the first and second fingers of the left hand above the fingerboard.

G ON THE 1ST STRING

ENSEMBLE

ODE TO JOY
(Theme from Symphony No. 9)

Slowly

Ludwig Van Beethoven

Count: 1 — 2 an 3 — 4

Study No. 43 (Melody) may be combined with Studies No. 62, 67 and 84.

ENSEMBLE

ANDANTE

Fernando Sor

Combine Study No. 44 (Melody) with Study No. 64 (Bass).

TEMPO MARKINGS

Tempo refers to the speed of the music. Various markings are used in music to indicate the tempo.

Largo	— Slow and broad
Andante	— Slow and even
Moderato	— A moderate tempo
Allegro	— Fast, quick
Vivace	— Lively, animated

TEMPO MARKINGS

ASS STRINGS

The 4th, 5th and 6th strings are the bass strings. Pluck the notes on these strings with the thumb using the st stroke. See explanation on right hand technique presented earlier in this book. Optional: the flat pick lectrum) could be used.

IEW NOTE — G

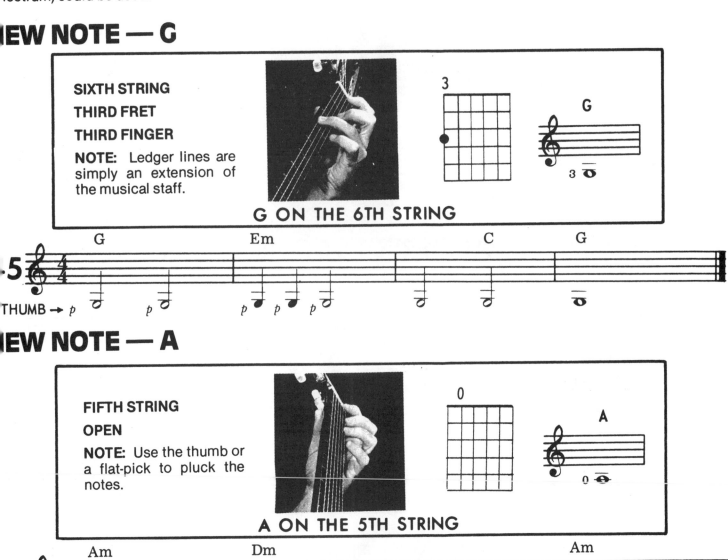

SIXTH STRING
THIRD FRET
THIRD FINGER

NOTE: Ledger lines are simply an extension of the musical staff.

G ON THE 6TH STRING

IEW NOTE — A

FIFTH STRING
OPEN

NOTE: Use the thumb or a flat-pick to pluck the notes.

A ON THE 5TH STRING

ENSEMBLE

NED'S BLUES

Combine Study No. 48 (Bass Part) with Study No. 31 (Melody).

NEW NOTE — B

FIFTH STRING
SECOND FRET
SECOND FINGER

B ON THE 5TH STRING

49

AT PIERROT'S DOOR

Traditional

NEW NOTE — C

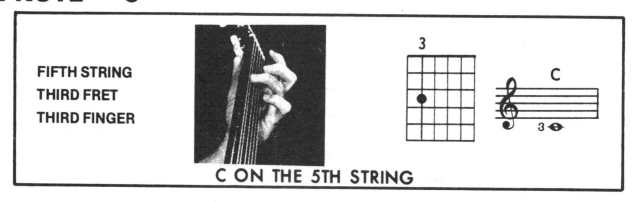

FIFTH STRING
THIRD FRET
THIRD FINGER

C ON THE 5TH STRING

51

52

MARY ANN (Trio)

Moderately, with a beat

Traditional

Count: 1 – 2 an 3   4

NEW NOTE — D

FOURTH STRING

OPEN

D

D ON THE 4TH STRING

ENSEMBLE

LITTLE BIRD (Bass Part)

Combine Study No. 56 (Bass Part) with Study No. 26 (Melody).

ROUND

NOTE: Second guitar(s) begin at letter **A** when first guitar(s) reaches letter **B**.

NOTE: Third guitar(s) begin at **A** when first guitar(s) reaches letter **C**.

NEW NOTE — E

FOURTH STRING
SECOND FRET
SECOND FINGER

E ON THE 4TH STRING

MARY'S THEME.

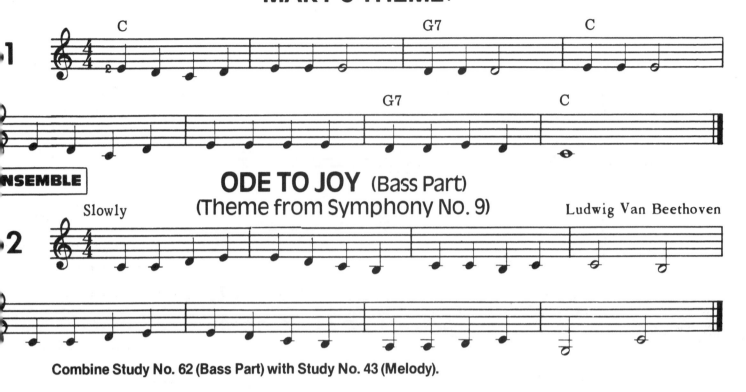

Combine Study No. 62 (Bass Part) with Study No. 43 (Melody).

EW NOTE — F

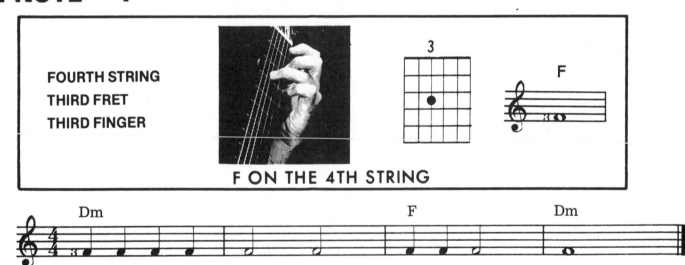

**FOURTH STRING
THIRD FRET
THIRD FINGER**

F ON THE 4TH STRING

ANDANTE (Bass Part)
(Segment)

Fernando Sor

Combine Study No. 64 (Bass Part) with Study No. 44 (Melody).

OLD JOE CLARK

Moderate

Tradition

65

ENSEMBLE

SYMPHONY No. 1 (Bass Part)
(Theme, Fourth Movement)

Slowly

Johannes Brahms

66

Combine Study No. 66 (Bass Part) with Study No. 40 (Melody).

ENSEMBLE

ODE TO JOY (Alto Part)

Slowly

Ludwig Van Beethov

67

Combine Study No. 67 (Alto Part) with Studies No. 43 (Melody) and 62 (Bass).

ERMATA

Hold and sustain the tone. Time value given to the tone(s) will depend on the music.

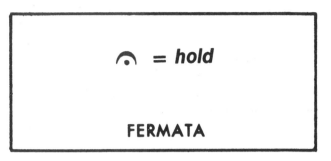

⌢ = *hold*

FERMATA

ENSEMBLE

DOXOLOGY
(Old Hundred)

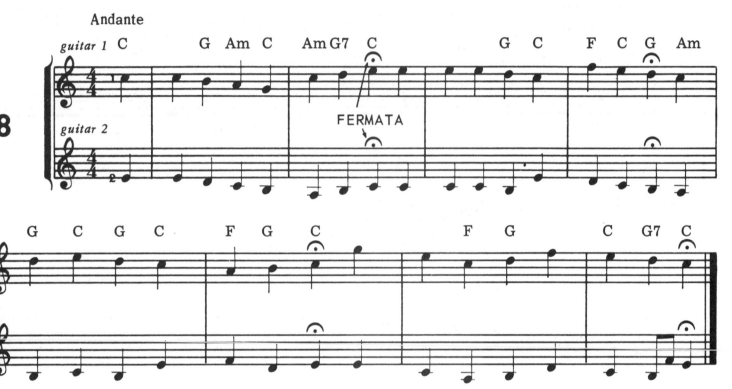

IRST AND SECOND ENDINGS

Quite often music repeats itself. First and second endings are used to save space.

ENSEMBLE

CHORALE No. 303

Johann Sebastian Bach

Study No. 69 may be combined with Study No. 82 (Bass Part).

88

SHARPS AND NATURALS

Sharps indicate to play the note ½ step higher — the distance of one fret. Naturals cancel Sharps.

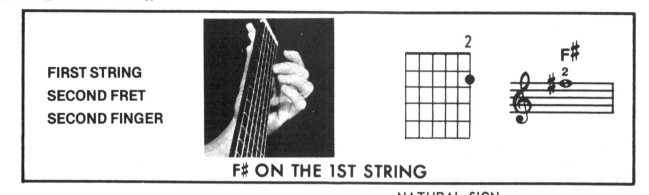

♯ = *a sharp raises the tone ½ step upward*

♮ = *a natural sign cancels the sharp*

SHARPS AND NATURALS

NEW NOTE — F♯

FIRST STRING
SECOND FRET
SECOND FINGER

F♯ ON THE 1ST STRING

70

NATURAL SIGN

CHOUCOUNE

Moderately

Anonymo

71

1 an — 2 an 3   4

SCALE — G MAJOR

The scale provides the skeleton upon which the melody of the song is based. The G major scale begins and ends on G.

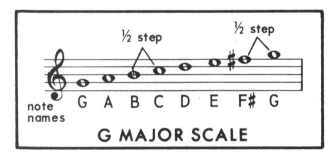

½ step   ½ step

note names   G A B C D E F♯ G

G MAJOR SCALE

Key Signature — Sharp all F's

72

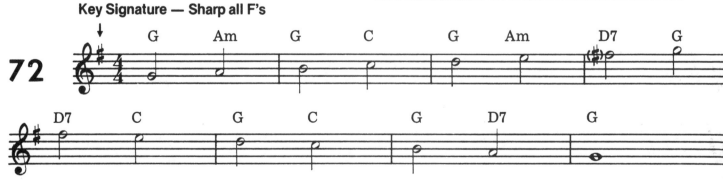

FOLK SONG

French

EW NOTE — F#

FOURTH STRING
FOURTH FRET
FOURTH FINGER

NOTE: Number in parentheses (3) equals alternate fingering.

F# ON THE 4TH STRING

ENSEMBLE

ALL THROUGH THE NIGHT

Traditional

NEW NOTES — E and F#

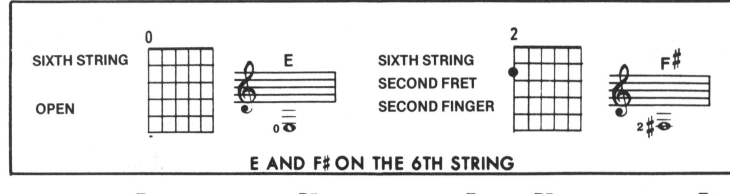

E AND F# ON THE 6TH STRING

JESU, JOY OF MAN'S DESIRING
(Alto and Bass Part)

Johann Sebastian Bach

Combine Study No. 77 (Alto and Bass) with Study No. 20 (Melody).

G SCALE

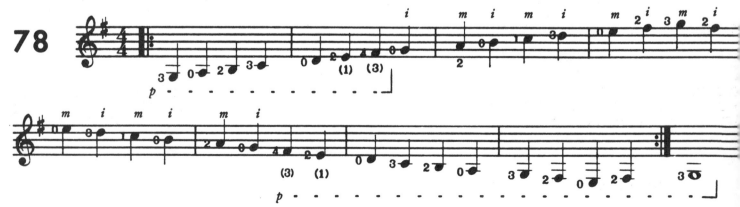

ORE SHARPS

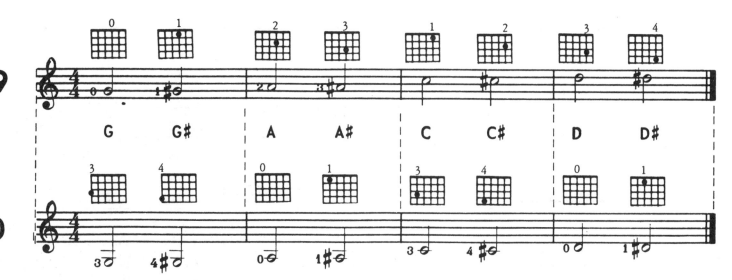

G   G#   A   A#   C   C#   D   D#

Studies No. 79 and 80 may be played together.

HROMATIC SCALE

A scale moving in half-steps is called a Chromatic Scale.
Memorize this scale and use it for warm-up.

CHORALE No. 303 (Bass Part)

NSEMBLE

Johann Sebastian Bach

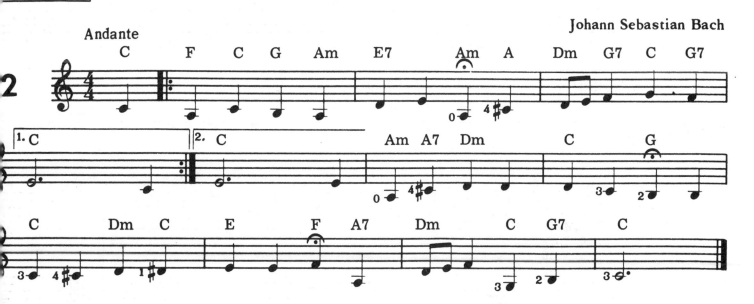

Combine Study No. 82 with Study No. 69 (Melody).

GREENSLEEVES (Duet)
(What Child Is This)

Traditional

ODE TO JOY (Optional Part)

Ludwig Van Beethoven

Combine Study No. 84 with Studies No. 43, 62 and 67 for a quartet.

ENSEMBLE

BOURREE

Johann Sebastian Bach

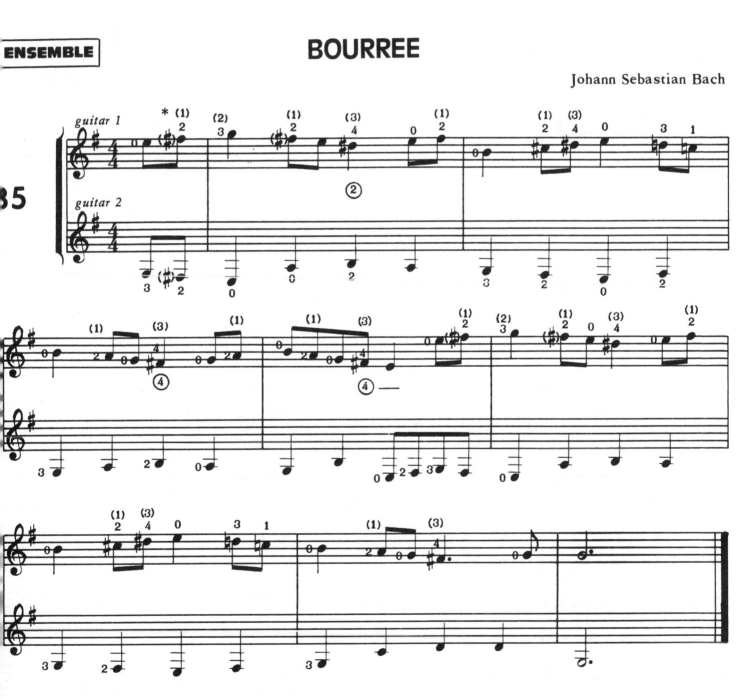

*NOTE: Alternate fingerings are indicated in parentheses.

NEW NOTE — A

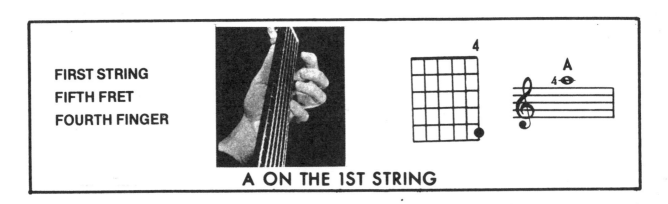

FIRST STRING
FIFTH FRET
FOURTH FINGER

A ON THE 1ST STRING

ENSEMBLE

DU, DU LIEGST MIR IM HERZEN
(You Live In My Heart)

German Folk Song

86

ENSEMBLE

HOUSE OF THE RISING SUN

Traditional

87

NOW THE DAY IS OVER

ENSEMBLE

Joseph Barnby

88

ENSEMBLE

SCARBOROUGH FAIR

Traditional

89

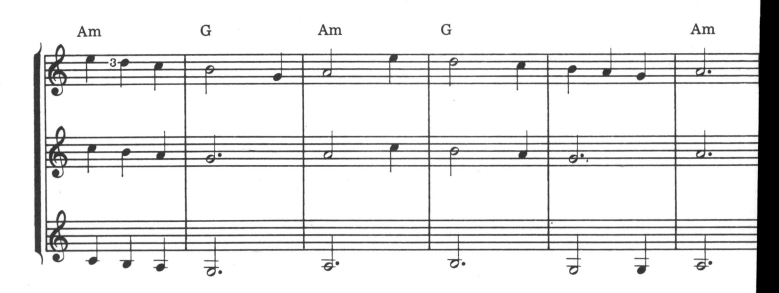